UNTOLD

Testimony and Guide to Overcoming Adversity

TRUE STORY WRITTEN BY

LEON FORD & LAQUINTE BRINSON

Published in Pittsburgh, Pennsylvania by Leon D. Ford

Photography and Book Design by Emmai Alaquiva
Ya Momz House, INC.

Untold, may be purchased in bulk for educational, business or sales promotional use. For more information email
sales@leonfordspeaks.com

For more information on how to book Leon Ford please email
booking@leonfordspeaks.com

Website:
www.leonfordspeaks.com

Follow Leon Ford on social media @Leonfordspeaks

TABLE OF CONTENTS

DEDICATION

This book is dedicated to everyone who has experienced, those who are currently experiencing or will experience some form of adversity in their lifetime. Remember that you are resilient; your life has value, and purpose regardless of what you may be experiencing at the moment. Please keep the faith, remain hopeful and remember that you are loved.

ACKNOWLEDGEMENTS

I would like to acknowledge my family and friends for the unconditional love and support. You all have fought with me, for me and you have had my back even when it seemed as if society had turned its back against me.

To the good experiences—and the bad for molding me into the leader that I am today. I embrace all of my lived experiences, as each moment is significant to my journey.

To those who have tragically lost their voices due to police violence—and their families, my voice is your voice and your voice is mine.

To the great leaders who have fought against systemic oppression and injustice before me—those who are currently fighting and those who will continue to fight after I am gone. Never give up!

To my supporters, those far and wide I sincerely appreciate you for sending your love, positive energy and for helping me to publicize my story.

Last but not least, I would like to acknowledge the creator for using me as a vessel to bring more hope, healing, positivity and love into the world.

With peace, love and spiritual guidance.

Thank you!

WORDS FROM JOHN EDGAR WIDEMAN

Leon— thank you for sharing your manuscript. I read it with great interest. Allowed what I'd read to sink in, then a week or so later re-read it. A second exposure reinforced my initial impression that you had accomplished something special in both the conception and execution of your project. I hope your book finds many readers or many readers find it. They will discover a unique, literal witness whose voice— unlike countless victims today and yesterday silenced forever by brutal police assaults— survives.

I also must admit, that during the first encounter with your script I had serious reservations. Not about your commitment, skills or intentions, but I worried that maybe you had chosen to ask the wrong person to write an introduction to your book. From the preface to epilogue your words acknowledge, praise and confirm the presence of God. Not only as an inspiration but as a co-conspirator and I don't share your belief in a divine, omniscient creator/maintainer of the cosmos.

Also, your book is organized as a sort of instructional manual. Complete with numbered lessons, poems, and biblical quotes to guide readers. I am extremely skeptical and suspicious of the genre of self-help, self-improvement, how-to succeed books which approach life's inevitable contradictions and paradoxes as problems resolvable in 3, 5, or 10 easy steps.

As I absorbed more deeply the significance, authenticity, profound witness captured by your voice. Our differing beliefs, different methods of communicating with readers, far from being an impediment, became motivation, impelling me to record a response.

The books I end up valuing most are often the ones I have to start and put down numerous times before I'm prepared to accept the challenge they present: to abandon my familiar world and enter unexplored terrain.

Of course, we are not strangers and have lots in common. We both grew up in Pittsburgh, and doesn't that make us homies of sorts, even if our birth dates are separated by more than half a century. The city has transformed itself drastically more than once during my lifetime.

As has the colored neighborhood that raised us. Still, it seems many of the glories, terrors, the lies and truths, promises and disappointments of Pittsburgh didn't change that much for the majority of its inhabitants— yesterday, or today. Especially, for the young people of color who suffer the same ole, same ole inequalities and deadly perils imposed upon them generation after generation.

Profound differences between the two of us were not exactly swept away by a second, closer reading of your text, yet the nature of the differences changed for me. Changed in the manner, you articulate so well when you describe how your anger, hate, desire for revenge changed. Or how you changed your attitude about assertions of doctors who declared with absolute certainty you would never walk again. One fact or truth is never simply replaced by another.

You demonstrate through word and deed that change is the nature of being human. Constant, unforeseeable change and difference. Evil perpetrated by cops who shot you five times, who ignored and mocked your pain and your utter helplessness. Who shackled you to a hospital bed although you were paralyzed and couldn't speak — all that evil, those facts cannot be undone, no more than facts doctors cited to you to confirm their dire predictions. You argue, however, that such facts or truths, no matter how cold, hard, unrelenting, need not necessarily define or confine a person.

Employing your case, for example, you insist an individual's power to change remains in their hands, despite or perhaps because of external circumstances. Even if the forces conspiring to usurp and control a person's identity (forces generated by what you call a "broken system") include state-sponsored police violence, economic and political marginality, cultural prejudice, systematic oppression, the vulnerability of mortal flesh and blood.

In her novel Their Eyes Were Watching God, Zora Neale Hurston announces, "To know there, you got to go there."This gem of folk wisdom Hurston draws from Afro-American oral tradition always reminds me of two things. First, my gratitude for the art of writing, the art of reading, the power of these arts to penetrate for a moment, illusory or not, the hard shell of who we are— our senses, our identity, personality— and allow the truth of another person to enter.

Second, I recall the immense distance imagination must navigate to reach things unknown. Knowledge is hard work. Great difficulty, as well as great distance, are implied by Hurston's aphorism. Particularly if the knowledge we are seeking is the sheer mystery, privacy, integrity, and implacability of another human being.

I believe both of us share a desire to go there and know there. To enter spaces that expand boundaries of the particular person we happen to be. Whether or not a seeker ever arrives, attempting to get there is a worthwhile task, and being on the road probably not a bad place to be. It's audacious, Leon, when you declare to other young people (old people, too) that they have a calling. Or when you address your peers with words like positive, honest, pure or entreat them not to allow social ills to change goodness inside or expect from every one of them righteousness, greatness.

I think you get away with saying such remarkable things and demanding that others take such unusual risks because you're able to convince your audience you have been there, done that. You stand before them as a reliable witness because you have paid dues of suffering. You have earned the understanding and wisdom revealed as you voice your pleas, tell your stories.

You define yourself as a spiritual being having a human experience, and your book illustrates how and why. Convinces readers that the most demanding inner struggle turns out to be the one waged against "principalities, powers, rulers of darkness in this world." You understand that without the support of warmth, love, and care you would not have survived an ordeal of prolonged, intense pain. It makes sense, even from my unbeliever's point of view, for you to assume the exceptional love, warmth, care that enabled your survival stands as yet another proof of the miraculous presence sustaining you daily.

I learned something new about patience and determination in the section you entitled,"Preparation." I was touched, humbled by the dimensions of your courage as you confronted obstacles— insurance companies, reluctant therapists and docs, bedsores, surgery— in a protracted, frustrating effort to procure RGO braces.

A harrowing story you tell, not because you're boasting, not because the tale ends happily with you in your new braces rising from a wheelchair and sprinting down a hospital corridor, But you relate the story to make the point that until we leave this earth, we all must deal with the unending, often cruel uncertainty life brings.

You offer no facile solutions. Instead, you show how the best part within each of us enables us to stay ready, primed for whatever reality serves up next. Your therapists were amazed by your familiarity with the exotic RGO braces the first day they (and you) strapped them on. Familiarity you had achieved quietly, privately during a period of discouraging setbacks when you studied descriptions of how the braces functioned, months before there seemed even a small chance they might arrive.

Good luck to you and your book. You offer a gift. May it be welcomed and appreciated.

John Edgar Wideman

THE POWER OF CONNECTION BY LAQUINTE' BRINSON

"What you create alone is impactful, but what we create together is powerful" – LaQuinte' Brinson

Imagine a connection so powerful that it invigorates you to reach a new dimension of greatness that transcends through your vision and helps change lives all over the world. When greatness collides, it becomes explosive, creating a force that will not be defeated by the oppositions of the journey. Connections of this magnitude are ordained by the Creator and should never be taken for granted.

It wasn't until I met Leon Ford that I understood the igniting power of connection. I discovered his story while scrolling through social media. I remember reaching out to Leon to ask him if he'd be willing to share his compelling story with my organization "The Break-Up, LLC." I was excited and eager to work with him. My vision was to interview Leon and write a blog about his story, but God had other plans.

When August 20, 2014, rolled around I was all set and ready for the interview. However, Leon informed me that earlier that day the judge over his case issued a gag order and he could no longer share his story until it was lifted. I decided at this moment that I would use my platform to share his story even if I didn't have a chance to interview him. I didn't understand what was happening at the time, but I now see that God would bless me with an extraordinary opportunity to help Leon to share his story.

Once Leon's trial was over, I flew out to Pittsburgh to meet him. As we sat and talked for hours, it felt like we had known each other our whole lives. Although we lived hundreds of miles away, we vowed to stay in contact with each other.

After several months passed Leon's gag order was lifted. On August

22, 2015, almost a year to the date when the gag order was issued, Leon flew out to Atlanta and accepted the 2015 Award of Inspiration and shared his story at the 2nd Anniversary Gala of The Break-Up, LLC. It was truly worth the wait and everyone left inspired after hearing his story.

With every encounter we became more connected, establishing a true friendship. Over time Leon and I began to realize that this was no ordinary connection, it wasn't like anything else we had experienced. It wasn't until we started writing the book that we understood that the Creator ordained our unorthodox relationship. God brought us into each other's lives and trusted us to release something powerful into the world. We didn't know what the journey would entail, but we were eager to get started.

Leon courageously unveiled himself of the social media filters, the public figure title, and his million-dollar smile so that he could reveal the untold. He trusted me with his deepest emotions and darkest moments so that we could create a paradigm for overcoming adversity.

As I began to coach him through the process, I discovered that I too was looking at Leon through the lenses of triumph, while having no real understanding of his trauma. I challenged myself as a life coach to remove all filters and barriers so that I could get to know Leon, the individual.

He began opening up, sharing what it is like to wake up every morning having to swing his legs out of bed to transfer into a wheelchair before starting his day. What it feels like to be robbed of his youth and innocence. What it's like raising his son in a society that doesn't value his life. What it's like to have people depending on him while simultaneously battling depression.

He shared with me how it feels to be a survivor who struggles daily to survive. The more time we spent writing the book, the more I got to know Leon. The process was very intense and emotional, challenging him to reach into pockets of darkness and pain revealing anguish that he desperately wanted to forget. There were moments when the pain was too great for him to express himself verbally, but his eyes told a story that words alone could not convey. His eyes told a story of exhaustion from the process of being optimistic when his circumstances screamed a different reality. His eyes told me that his mind never has an opportunity to rest because it's trying to figure out how to break free from all of the chaos. His eyes showed me that champions feel like giving up too.

Through his vulnerability and transparency untold was birthed. We spent countless hours together writing this book. I now understand that the one that's always pushing needs a push sometimes too. The one who's helping others heal has broken pieces too. The one that's fighting for justice needs the judicial system to fight for him. Through this process, I've become a better life coach, mentor, and friend understanding that with life comes trauma, pain, and purpose.

I will never underestimate the power of connection and what two people can create when they come together. If I tried to share with you the magnitude of power that encompassed the writing experience it would be an entirely separate book. But I will close with this.

If I were ever limited to one thing to prove to someone that God is real, I'd introduce them to Leon Ford. If I had to explain God's grace, I'd use his life as an example. If I need a visual of strength, I'd ask him to smile. If I needed inspiration, I'd read his book over and over again. That's how powerful Leon's story is. God has used Leon Ford as a vessel to help me to understand who He is on a deeper level.

I am amazed how so much purpose has come from so much pain. His story will be used to help heal the world. I was immensely blessed while helping Leon to write his story and I am confident that you will be profoundly blessed as you read it.

Leon, Thank you for trusting me to help you to share your story with the world. I am forever grateful.

"What you create alone is impactful, but what we create together is powerful" - **LaQuinte' Brinson**

FOREWORD BY STEPHEN DEBERRY

The universe works in mysterious ways.

Two years ago I flew to Washington, D.C. to give a talk to a group of remarkable men who had gathered in the nation's Capitol to celebrate and deepen their leadership efforts in communities across the country. My talk that day was about the lessons I'd learned over the years as an anthropologist, business person, and adventure traveler. The goal of the talk was to share observations and experiences I hoped would be of some use to the men who were and are "doing the work." I had the good sense to know that I could learn as much from them (and probably more) than I had to offer. I just didn't know exactly what I would learn, or how. Then I met Leon Ford.

What I would say most about meeting Leon is that I was startled. As I learned of his story I was startled by the brutishness with which he was treated by the police; disturbed by the fact that this young man was shot five times and relegated to live in a wheelchair. I was startled by the ways in which the workings of the criminal justice system conspired with malice, laziness, and apathy to peck and peel at the constitution of an innocent man. As I got to know Leon, what startled me most were the unexpected and uplifting ways that Leon remained unscathed, graceful, and hopeful in elegant defiance of the injustices blanketing him. A lesser person--that is to say, any normal person -- may have collapsed under the same conditions. Not Leon Ford.

We became friends, checking in on each other from time to time over text messages or the occasional phone call. One day our paths were set to intersect in ways I couldn't have anticipated.

I suffered a severe spinal chord injury, at the hands of an overly-aggressive chiropractor, of all things. I was relegated to lay motionless on my back for months. I couldn't walk around freely.

I couldn't sit upright. I was prescribed narcotics to get through the pain while simultaneously seeing daily warnings in the news about opioid addiction. I felt trapped. I couldn't lift my baby girls at home, or play in our big summer water balloon fight as they'd so looked forward to. I was forced to sit still in excruciating pain and just think about it. I went from being a national champion athlete, a mountain climber, surfer and explorer to hearing myself have to utter the words "I am disabled" while trying to plead my case for help as I made my way through the airport in a wheelchair. My emotions tumbled: anger, resentment, loneliness.

It wasn't my focus at the time, but I now realize I was getting a tiny taste of what Leon Ford must have experienced. I do mean a small taste since despite my many torments I didn't have to deal with the trappings of the criminal justice system. Despite the severity of my injury, I knew that I should be able to recover near-fully. For these reasons and more I have a particular appreciation for Leon's story.

One evening, not long after I'd initially been injured, I was at home late at night with my wife. It was time for bed, but I felt a strange sense that I wasn't supposed to be at home. In a way that is hard to explain I felt -- no, I knew -- I was supposed to be somewhere else. I followed my gut and called Pastor Paul Bains in East Palo Alto to ask if he had an empty bed in the shelter he runs. I wasn't sure exactly why, but somehow I knew that was where I was supposed to be that night. There happened to be an empty bed that evening, and Pastor Bains invited me to take it. I accepted.

I made my way to the shelter alone wearing a Cervical neck brace. I laid mostly awake in a cot that evening, staring mostly at the ceiling because I couldn't move my head. I listened more than usual. I could hear some of my new roommates snore while others talk in their sleep or get up to go to the bathroom. Despite our physical closeness, I realized I didn't know most of them, and reciprocally, most had no idea who I was. The grand irony of it all was we were all there in that tiny space, and despite all of us having things to offer each other, most of us remained anonymous, which meant our collective learning was squandered. This is the problem with untold stories.

I spent the morning after my slumber in the shelter in silent reflection. I thought about what I'd seen and how I felt. I thought about how important it is for all of us to nurture empathy, not just for the benefit of others, but also for our well-being. I thought about how important it is to know each other's stories. I thought about Leon, and the powerful example he has become. And then, as if on cue, a text message flashed across my phone screen. It was Leon Ford. We hadn't been in touch for a while. He was asking reaching out to ask if I would write the foreword to his book. True story. I told you the universe works in mysterious ways.

As I write these words, I am now two weeks past a spine surgery that has restored my ability to walk about, but I still can't lift my children or throw water balloons. I am still working through my feelings of loss and toward forgiveness for the person who hurt me. Along the way, the words in Leon's book have been useful to me. I genuinely believe they can be of use to you, too.

Stephen DeBerry
September 19, 2017

Leon Ford's Testimony and Guide to Overcoming Adversity

WRITTEN BY LEON FORD AND LAQUINTE' BRINSON

UNTOLD

A LETTER FROM MY MOM

My son, Leon Ford, born March 16, 1993, has always been charismatic, courageous, and resilient. Since he was a child, Leon had a magnetizing personality to complement his infectious smile, which could brighten anyone's day. I remember giving birth to my precious son. He immediately brought joy into my world. His father and I knew that God had blessed us immensely from the moment we laid our eyes on him. I was overwhelmed with joy and gratitude that God chose me to bring forth such an amazing gift to share with the world. I knew without a doubt that God had created someone special, but I had no idea of all he would have to endure throughout his life.

The morning of November 11, 2012, I woke up to a worrisome phone call from Leon's father, Leon Ford Sr. I could hear the concern in his voice as he asked me if I had heard from our son. Neither of us had spoken to Leon, and his father was worried because Leon had not come home the night before. Leon hadn't communicated his whereabouts to anyone in the family. Initially, I wasn't worried; I was optimistic and suggested that Leon might have fallen asleep at his grandmother's house, or perhaps he'd stayed with another friend or relative. We called numerous family members and friends, but no one was able to provide any information about where Leon stayed that night. I began to worry; it was unlike my son not to let anyone know where he would be. After numerous attempts to locate our son, something in my spirit told me to contact the local auto pound to see if his car might have been towed.

I learned my son's car had been impounded. I was baffled, and I immediately asked why his car was impounded, but the secretary informed me that she could not give me any information because the car was under investigation. I felt sick, and my heart dropped into my stomach. It felt as if I was on the world's fastest roller coaster, on a downward spiral without a seatbelt.

I had no idea why my son's car would have been impounded or why there would be an open investigation. I frantically attempted to call Leon's father to inform him that Leon's car was impounded and under investigation. To my surprise, my phone began to ring; we were calling each other simultaneously. As I answered my cell, I heard Leon Sr. screaming at the top of his lungs. "They shot my son, they shot my son! Somebody saw his car on the news. The police shot our son." My soul was shaken to the core. I wailed, "Noooo," and hung up.

I remember praying to God, asking him to spare my son's life. I cried out and said, "Lord, please protect my child. You promised not to give me more than I could handle. I cannot lose another child—oh God, please." My knees were weak and I felt as if I might collapse. However, that didn't stop me from rushing to the hospital to care for my son. I prayed many prayers as I sped off to the hospital. I wanted nothing more than for my son to be alive.

I arrived at the hospital, and I ran inside, thinking I would soon be comforting my son. I wanted him to feel my presence, even if he were unconscious. I wanted to tell him to be strong and to inform him that his family was by his side, but that didn't happen. The staff at the information desk said that they did not have a Leon Ford at this particular hospital.

I pleaded with the secretary, nurses, and hospital security for any information regarding my son, but they continued to tell me forcefully that they didn't have anyone registered under his name. I felt completely helpless. Family members went to other hospitals in the area and were also told that there was no patient named Leon Ford. My heart was completely broken, and I burst into tears because I thought my son was dead. I was told he was not at any hospital, so I thought the only place he could be was the county morgue.

I cried and cried. I prayed to God, and I prayed to my daughter Leona, who had been tragically killed when she was hit by a truck at the age of ten. I cried out, "Please, baby, protect your brother. I need you to release all the angels in heaven so they can cover Leon and give him the strength to survive."

With the grace of God, Leon survived being unjustly shot five times by a Pittsburgh police officer during a traffic stop. However, our lives have never been the same since November 11, 2012. Not only was Leon shot five times and robbed of his ability to walk, but he was also charged with numerous offenses he did not commit. Our family was devastated by this news, but Leon has managed to turn tragedy into triumph.

Leon's testimony about overcoming such great adversities is confirmation of what I felt the day I gave birth to him. I knew there was something extraordinary about him. His strength, determination, and resilience pulled him through some of his lowest moments. And he continues to push through the pain daily, never giving up, no matter how difficult his circumstances.

I cannot express my gratitude to God for sparing my son's life. Not only did he give my son the strength to survive, but he also gave him the courage to speak for those who are unable to speak for themselves, the tenacity to overcome all adversity thrown his way, and the wisdom to lead from a place of purpose. He is a living embodiment of courage, using his story to positively impact all lives. As a mother, I cannot express how proud I am to witness my son turn a tragic story into a testimony of love, compassion, and understanding.

Untold contains many stories of Leon's personal experiences, along with his insights on how we can all overcome adversity. I have applied many of the lessons from this book to my life. What makes this book so great is that anyone can apply these teachings to their lives so they can overcome adversity and have a positive impact on society.

Latonya Green

PREFACE

I have found an innovative way to not only tell my story of police brutality but to also offer my story as a guide to help readers overcome adversity through faith and spiritual growth. I know that what I experienced is much bigger than me, so I am compelled to share the lessons that I've learned throughout the most painful moments of my life. You will find that in each entry this book offers a title, quote, personal story, lesson, and a daily shift, followed by affirmation. In each story, you will get to know in detail what I experienced as a survivor of police brutality. You will also find insight into what enabled me to overcome this tragic moment and helped me to heal physically, emotionally, and spiritually. I suggest you read the stories chronologically. Be sure to apply each lesson to your life by implementing the daily shifts so that you can make this transformation.

INTRODUCTION

Often I am asked, how do you continue to smile through all of your pain? How do you stay positive? Why haven't you given up? What keeps you going? For a long time, I didn't know how to answer those questions. I didn't understand why I was smiling and why I hadn't given up. I didn't even know where the strength to keep going and to keep smiling came from.

The pain hasn't gone away; it still hurts at this very moment. The tears haven't dried up; I cry often, and I still experience pain. I still have to look at the hurt in my parents' eyes when they see me every day, knowing that my life is forever changed. From the outside looking in, people see peace, forgiveness, grace, and strength, but they are unaware of the struggles that I face within.

For years, it felt like there was a war going on inside of my mind. The war inside of my mind was even more draining than what I was experiencing physically. I honestly wanted the negative emotions to win the battle so that I could retaliate with anger and hatred. I wanted others to feel pain because I was in pain, but I felt in my heart that wasn't right.

What I felt in my heart was so strong that it didn't allow me to retaliate. Even in the midst of pain, I believed that things would somehow get better. I was optimistic.

A force within spoke to me and revealed to me that my life had meaning, that my life was purposeful, and that I would have a positive impact on people all over the world. I now know that the magnitude of the pain I have experienced was a part of my journey to evolve into who the Creator wanted me to be.

While writing this book, I began to understand my process on a deeper level, and it has opened my eyes to my spiritual journey.

This spiritual journey has shown me that God used all the pain I've experienced to develop me into a vessel that will lead people to Him.

Through this experience, I became dedicated to sharing my story and changing lives in an unconventional way. I've never been a religious person. I didn't grow up in the church, and I never had a desire to go. But I always had a desire to strengthen my relationship with God.

I started this book to tell my story, but the process of sharing my story has turned into a ministry. Every word of this book ministered to me and has fed my spirit. Writing this book has strengthened my relationship with God. I am hoping that my story can minister to you and help you strengthen your relationship with God as well. I know that we all have many different beliefs systems and some may not believe at all. However, I am asking for you to be open minded as a share my testimony with you.

Throughout this book, I share some of the darkest and loneliest moments of my process. I now realize that I was never alone. I remember feeling utterly hopeless. I felt like my life had no importance, like I was here for no reason at all. I was empty, and it felt like every ounce of life was taken from me.

When I was told I was paralyzed, my soul was completely broken. Life as I knew it was over. Only one thing had the power to save my life, and that was my faith in God. I was completely disconnected from the conventional way of communicating with God, but he found me exactly where I was.

There was a time when I didn't know how to pray. I was never taught the traditional way of praying. But I now understand that I was always in communication with God. A "gut feeling" is the best way that I know to explain this communication. There was a time when I would only listen to my "gut feeling," but I now communicate with it. I now know my "gut feeling" is my open line of communication with God.

Through my open line of communication with God, I can better understand my spirit and my process which helps me to better understand how I can smile through all of the pain. My smile brings comfort and healing, and that's why I'm able to push through the pain.

My positive energy is a magnetic force that transcends to those around me, no matter their adversity. Although I have lost so much and have experienced a great deal of pain, my spirit is pure and receptive to the purpose that God has for my life. My spiritual journey has given me insight. Revealing to me that although society failed me and caused me to endure an astronomical amount of physical, emotional, and mental pain, my life still has purpose.

Through all the pain that I have experienced, I am still pushing to thrive and live a purposeful life. When society wrote me off as just another black kid whose life had no value, God gave me a platform that has allowed me to use my voice to raise awareness, create positive change, and promote healing and inspiration.

As I share with you many of my untold stories of pushing through the pain, I pray that God will open your heart and your mind so your spirit is also fed through the words He has given me.

Anger

> Anger is the most impotent of passions. It effects nothing
> it goes about, and hurts the one who is possessed by it
> more than the one against whom it is directed.
>
> —Carl Sandburg

The shooting left me clinging to life, and I had to undergo multiple surgeries to stay alive. When I awoke, I was heavily sedated and in excruciating pain. I was unable to speak. There were tubes in my mouth. The officers had shackled me to the bed with cuffs, and they surrounded me, as if I could get up and leave the hospital.

The doctors came in the room, and they began explaining the surgeries they had performed; they also informed me about my spinal cord injury. One of the five bullets had pierced my spine, resulting in paralysis. I was unable to respond to them or ask questions. After the surgeries, I was utterly confused about my overall condition. But in my heart, I was grateful to be alive.

I remember being in intensive care. The room was dark, cold and my surroundings were completely unfamiliar. As I gazed around the small room I immediately noticed the noisy machines positioned directly next to my bed.

These machines connected strange tubes and wires to my wounded body and made my room seem ten times smaller. I was unsure if my family knew I had been shot or if they were aware of where I was. I wanted so badly to see my family; I wanted them to know I was alive, that I needed their love and needed them to be my voice.

My parents had already lost a child—my sister Leona, who was tragically killed when she was ten years old. I remember the pain, the toll her death took on my family, and I didn't want them to experience the pain of losing another child.

The high dosages of medication made it difficult to stay awake. One moment I was looking around, thinking deeply about life. I constantly thought about my sister and her death. I could not help but reflect on the physical pain I was experiencing. I sat and wondered how long it would take before I could breathe on my own. I just wanted to escape the pain and be healed. I gazed at my morphine drip, patiently waiting for the pain to go away. Before I knew it, I would fade out and fall asleep.

I had no concept of time. I was enraged about what had happened to me and that I was treated like a criminal. There was no comfort, love, or any emotional support. I desperately needed my family, but they couldn't be there for me. I wanted the tubes removed so I could ask if my family knew where I was or if they had tried to see me. I just wanted to know what was going on.

Why was I shackled to the bed? I had just come out of extensive surgery, I couldn't breathe independently, and several pints of blood flowed into my body. Due to the pain, my body was in complete shock. I was in critical condition fighting for my life.

I remember lying in bed one day when the news came on—to my surprise, I saw my family. I was happy and relieved, but the officer immediately turned off the TV before I had an opportunity to hear them speak. Being denied the right to listen to what my family had to say left me furious. But I had no way of communicating my feelings; the tubes prevented me from talking, so I was forced to remain in my thoughts.

I thought about how badly I hated police officers. I wanted them to feel pain, and I wanted them to suffer for what they had done to me. I felt tons of anger toward the officers. I wanted them to know that I hated them. With no way to express my feelings, I became consumed by my thoughts, which pulled me deeper into a pit of anger and rage.

As the days went on, my desire to receive comfort and love grew more intense. I stared at the TV for hours, desperately hoping I would see my family again and hear what they were saying. Unfortunately, that opportunity never returned. But one story aired on the news about two young men who made a rap song expressing their anger toward the police. As I was watching the news, I realized I had grown up with them.

The lyrics were expressive and painted a clear picture of their pain and rage. They were publicly ridiculed, charged with making terroristic threats and with witness intimidation. The charges filed were a direct result of their violently expressed lyrics aimed toward local police officers. One of the officers would potentially testify in court. The two received prison sentences as a result of their lyrics. The expression of their feelings toward the police validated how I was feeling. For the very first time, I felt like I had a voice.

After seeing the penalties they received for expressing their pain my anger intensified. I realized that society expected me to endure my great pain privately. The consequences experienced by those young men revealed to me that public expression of my pain would only lead to increased pain for both me and my family.

I became imprisoned by anger. I went so long without being able to speak because I had tubes down my throat. The only way I could express myself was through tears. It even became painful to cry because the residue from the tears built up around my eyes turning into crust.

Whenever my tears would dry, more tears would come. Tears nearly tattooed my face reminding me of a stray dog at an animal shelter. No one showed me love. I felt like an animal. My thoughts of revenge became more disturbing as my frustration grew.

Circumstances didn't provide me with an opportunity to speak, but I used my silence to my advantage. I spent time sorting through the voice in my head, learning the value of processing information before conveying my thoughts and feelings. My lack of expression taught me to be patient, wise, and strategic when dealing with my emotions. I learned to silence my mind, which gave me the ability to become more sensitive to my spirit.

Although I was furious, I was spiritually open to knowledge, understanding, and wisdom. Being receptive to my soul helped me to free myself from hatred, confusion, and conflict even while experiencing some of the most painful and spiritually challenging moments in my life.

I thought about great leaders who had also faced injustice; they spoke strategically, with wisdom and thoughtfulness. Their understanding of dealing with emotions appropriately enabled them to more efficiently express their emotions. These leaders successfully led movements, despite controversy.

During the extended period I was unable to speak, I learned the significance of using my voice. Being unable to talk taught me to speak with thoughtfulness, not just from my emotions. Speaking from a place of anger without strategy leads to confusion and greater pain. Anger without wisdom is nothing more than chaos. Creating a chaotic environment in the midst of a painful situation prevents healing and forward movement. When we express anger with a strategy, we become open to finding solutions by using the same culprit that caused us pain.

You will encounter situations that will result in anger, but you don't have to react to the feeling. What painful situations have you experienced in your life that has led to anger? How has anger influenced your process?

It is imperative to remain mindful when expressing your feelings. Anger often pacifies your pain for the moment, but it doesn't offer any solutions and can become disruptive to your healing process. The expression of anger often leads to controversy, but it doesn't have to be chaotic. Using wisdom while expressing your anger keeps you from causing more pain to both yourself and others.

Responding with anger is the natural response to pain, but you must challenge yourself on a greater level by pulling purpose from your pain. Pulling meaning from pain helps you take power away from anger. This allows you to navigate in your purpose by finding solutions to the pain in a graceful manner. Navigating in your purpose gives you more power than what has harmed you.

Daily Shift

As you deal with painful situations that result in anger, implement the following daily shifts:

1. Pray for understanding of what has harmed you.
2. Seek wisdom through meditation.
3. Privately strategize the most positive and effective way to express yourself.
4. Pull purpose from your pain, and remember that your purpose has more power than your pain.

Affirmation

I will control my anger;
My anger will not control me.
I will control my thoughts;
My thoughts will not control me.
I refuse to cause pain to myself and others.
I will express my anger with wisdom.
I will express my anger with understanding.
I will express my anger with peace.
My anger is controlled.
My pain is purposeful.
I will be peaceful.
I will be patient.
I will be wise.
I will be strategic.
I will be thoughtful.
I am open to solutions.

GOD'S GRACE

Even in your lowest moments, when you have no control over anything and your faith is weak, God's grace is sufficient.

My initial response to the pain I experienced was anger. I was angry because a police officer unjustly shot me. I was angry because when I woke up from surgery, the first person I saw was an officer—the last person I wanted to see after such a horrific experience. I was petrified.

Although I was on a breathing machine and could barely move, my mind went into a panic because I didn't know if the officer in front of me was the same officer who shot me. I didn't know if that person would attempt to hurt me again.

I was angry because I couldn't speak; there was no way to let anyone know how badly the officers treated me. I was angry because I had no way to contact my family. I later found out that they were restricted from visiting me and weren't given any information about my condition. I was angry because I was experiencing an unfathomable amount of mental, physical, and emotional pain. I was also mad at God for allowing me to face such great injustice.

At that point, I thought to myself, *if God is real, why is He allowing this to happen to me?* Then I wondered if I should ask God why. Was I wrong for asking him why? I didn't communicate with God regularly, so I didn't know how to feel or what to believe.

In the midst of these thoughts, I was surrounded by hatred. The officers in my room saw the tears rolling down my face; they saw the dried blood splattered all over my body; they saw that I was experiencing a tremendous amount of pain.

16

Any human being would've had compassion for another in my condition. However, those officers were completely cold and had no empathy for my life. I was clinging on to the little bit of life that I had left, and I had no one by my side to offer emotional support.

The doctors were uncertain if I would survive, even after they performed multiple surgeries. The pain was nearly unbearable, and I didn't know how much longer I could hold on. While experiencing that pain, I wanted to sleep all day. Waking up was painful. I felt as if I had broken every single bone in my body. The bullet holes in my arm, chest, neck, and hip burned, as if someone was cutting me slowly with a knife soaked in alcohol.

Although I was conscious, the tubes down my throat prevented me from speaking, which brought a significant amount of frustration. Doctors poked me with needles. Bright lights and beeping noises made it almost impossible for me to sleep.

I remember how badly I wanted to be home with my family. While experiencing the all-encompassing pain, all I could think about was how badly I wanted to feel the warmth of my mother's touch or the comfort of my father's protection. I was heartbroken.

Every time I fell asleep, I expected my parents to be in my room when I woke up, but they never were. As negative emotions overtook me, I kept replaying the voices of the officers wishing me death as they stood over my bullet-riddled body. I lay in a puddle of my blood, not knowing if another shot would be fired, ending my life.

The officers in the room felt no remorse for all the pain they put me through; I as if felt they were awaiting my death. Because of the tube down my throat, suction was necessary to remove saliva and prevent me from choking. I had no mobility in my left arm, so I used my right arm to place the suction in my mouth. Once when I extended my hand toward my mouth with the suction, I accidentally dropped it.

I began frantically reaching for the suction, but I was unable to grab it. I started choking; I shook my head from side to side, trying to drain the saliva from my mouth, but it didn't work. I banged on the bed with my right arm to get the attention of the officer in the room. He looked at me, turned his back to me, and turned the volume up on the television. I was panicking, unable to breathe.

Once again I was extremely close to death. The hatred radiated from the officer's body and surrounded the room. I felt completely helpless and defeated by yet another adversity. Just as I thought I was taking my last breath, a nurse came in to provide assistance. Ultimately, she helped save me from choking to death.

I lay on the ground, blood oozing from my mouth and gasping for air, and God spared my life. As the surgeons cut my body open in a desperate attempt to save me, God guided them through every procedure. As I lay in pain, wishing for the comfort of my family, the presence of God surrounded me. When, in an excruciating amount of pain, I was ready to give up, God gave me strength. And as the officers wished me death, God gave me life.

I was not thinking about God, nor was I focused on his grace. But I now understand that it was God's grace that pulled me through. God's grace served as confirmation that he was with me throughout my lowest moments. When hatred surrounded me, the grace of God protected me from evil.

Even in your lowest moments, when you have no control over anything and your faith is weak, God's grace is sufficient. Even in your most painful moments, when it feels like God doesn't exist, when you question if God is real, and when you continually ask God why, He will nurture you. He'll guide you through the pain.

There may come a time in your life when you don't have the ability to use your voice to talk to God, but his grace is responsive to your needs. When hatred surrounds you, the presence of God always protects and sustains you. We must let go of the things that we can't control and allow God's grace to serve us. It is essential that we keep God's grace and the presence of God in the forefront of our lives as we push through the pain.

Daily Shift

As you go throughout your day, focus on God's grace by implementing the following daily shifts:

1. Identify God's grace and the presence of God as you push through the pain.
2. Do not consume yourself with the hatred surrounding you.
3. You must be sensitive to the confirmation of God's grace.
4. Let go of the things you can't control, and allow God's grace to serve you.

Affirmation of Grace

God's grace is sufficient.
Even in my lowest moments God's grace will pull me through.
I am sensitive to the confirmation of God's grace.
God's grace is responsive to my needs.
Even when I am surrounded by hatred, the presence of God keeps me safe.
I will acknowledge God's grace as I push through the pain.

LIMITATIONS

Faith is having nothing but knowing that you have everything.

Within the first few days in the hospital, I learned I was paralyzed. I remember the doctor coming into my hospital room and flashing a light in my eyes to see if I was awake. I still had tubes down my throat, so I couldn't speak. I was limited to blinking my eyes and shaking my head.

The doctor asked if I could hear him, and I responded by nodding my head up and down to signal that I could hear him. The doctor proceeded to say that he had good news and he had bad news. "The good news is that you are going to survive; the bad news is that a bullet hit your spine, and you will never walk again."

Those piercing words instantly sent chills throughout my entire body. However, I didn't respond in the way that most would expect. At the time, I was high on the medications administered to help me cope with the pain. The medications helped me sleep, but I remained in constant agony from the excruciating pain. It felt like I had fallen off of a building and landed on my chest.

It was extremely painful to breathe, so I held my breath as long as I possibly could to relieve myself of the pain I experienced—with every breath I took.

With limited mobility in my left arm from the gunshot wound, I was left with a throbbing, numb sensation that never subsided. The pain wasn't only physical; it was also emotionally draining.

All of the news concerning my physical condition was bad, and the pain I felt intensified. I literally wanted to die because the pain was nearly too great to bear. It didn't seem real; it felt like a horrible dream I would soon awake from. I was unable to physically react to the news because I could only move my eyes and my right arm.

My emotions were trapped inside of me, and my thoughts were consumed by the negative limitations the doctors placed on my circumstances. The doctors tried their best to help me; however, the news that I would never walk again was devastating.

I knew that I would never accept the idea that I would never be able to stand up or walk, but the doctors crushed all hope by telling me that it was impossible. Initially, I wasn't sure if I would survive or not; therefore, it was more crucial to focus on survival than my ability to walk.

I was in the ICU for almost a month. I knew that I would survive. Once I made the transition into a regular room, I began to get stronger. I no longer had tubes down my throat; the staples were removed from my body, and I was able to eat regular food.

My physical progression took several weeks but it was faster than doctors expected, considering the severity of my injuries. That led me to believe that I would soon make a full recovery. However, the daily reminders of the limitations I was faced with left me emotionally drained.

I wasn't able to get in and out of the bed on my own. I wasn't able to use the bathroom independently. Nor was I able to stand and look my family and friends in their eyes. These were small things that I once took for granted, and I desperately longed for the abilities of my past.

Having to confront my new reality was very discouraging, and my faith weakened and confirmed the limitations the doctors placed on my condition. I tried everything in my power to block out the pain mentally. My mental numbness served as a coping mechanism, which made it even more difficult for me to accept my daunting condition.

I couldn't seem to wrap my mind around the permanence of my prognosis, and I honestly believed that I would get better. As time went on, I realized that it wasn't a nightmare—it was my reality. Although it was my reality and I was forced to come to grips with being unable to walk, I refused to allow my physical limitations to render me unfaithful to God and his ability to heal me.

While dealing with the pain of it all, I begin to consult other physicians. Doctor after doctor repeated the same piercing words: "You will never walk again." Hearing those words over and over left me emotionally depleted. After the fourth doctor, I recall having a complete breakdown because each doctor had failed me.

I began to understand that I needed a miracle. And no doctor could perform the miracle I needed. Therefore the miracle had to come from God. At that moment, I realized I was putting my faith in the wrong individuals. I began to understand that it was essential for me to have confidence in myself, and most importantly, to have faith in God.

In life, there will be people who place their limitations on you. They will tell you what you can and cannot do, based on their perspectives of who you are, your circumstances, and their personal beliefs. However, you must remember that you are a child of God, and anything is possible when you remain faithful. You must believe that everything will work out; you must embrace the process.

God doesn't always heal your brokenness in the time frame you think you should be healed. However, just because God doesn't operate on your timeline doesn't mean that it isn't in His plan. Therefore, we must see beyond the limitations others place on us, as well as the limitations we put on ourselves.

If we're not careful, we will allow the limitations others place on us to become the threshold of our faith. You must believe beyond what you can see and what others say. Faith is having nothing but knowing that you have everything. Your circumstances don't determine your destiny.

Daily Shift

As you go through your day, remain steadfast in your faith by implementing the following daily shifts:

1. Don't internalize the limitations that others place on you.
2. Be mindful of who and what you have faith in.
3. Be persistent in your pursuit of what you believe.
4. Trust God's timing.

Affirmation of Faith

I refuse to internalize the limitations of others.
My faith in God is all I need.
I believe beyond what others think.
I believe beyond what I can see.
My circumstances do not determine my destiny.
I am strong.
I am resilient.
I am limitless.

FEAR

Your willingness to win must be stronger than your fear of the pain.

Being hospitalized for an extended period was necessary for the level of trauma that I'd experienced, but it took a major toll on my body. I spent nearly five months in the hospital, and for approximately two of those months I was on bed rest. When I was shot, both of my lungs collapsed; in efforts to save my life I had a sternotomy, a procedure that involved surgically opening my sternum to treat internal wounds. They opened my chest by sawing through my sternum. As a result, I was on sternum precaution for months, which prevented me from lifting heavy objects or sitting in an upright position.

Although I was in a terrible place physically, suffering lots of pain for several months, I was grateful for the things that brought any sense of normalcy to my life. I no longer woke up to officers guarding my room, and I was free from the unnecessary shackles that had confined me to the bed. That brought me great relief.

I not only felt a sense of freedom, but I felt like a human being. I was surrounded by the love and comfort of my friends and family. After several weeks of being tube fed, I was finally able to eat solid foods again. Through gratitude, I found a sense of comfort under very uncomfortable circumstances.

My life had taken a drastic downward turn, but I was grateful to be alive. I was grateful for my family, and I was grateful for their unwavering love. I knew that my circumstance would eventually get better, but I was fearful of what was to come. From all of the surgeries, I was stitched and stapled to seal the wounds. But to completely heal, I had to endure the painful processes when the doctors removed the tubes, stitches, and staples from my body.

Fragments of the bullets that violently tore through my flesh painfully remained trapped inside of my body. The doctors said that removing the bullets would be more dangerous than leaving them, so I was faced with the reality of having foreign metal in me forever. Getting better was painful, but I knew that I had to go through the pain to be healed.

One day, the doctors came in to help me sit up for the very first time. When they swung my legs off the bed, I immediately started experiencing spasms. They lifted my upper body with a strap until finally my entire body was upright. My eyes went black, and my spasms were so intense that my whole body shook vigorously. I thought that I was having a seizure because I had no control over my body.

The entire time I had a horrific headache; I was dizzy and nauseous, and I pleaded with the doctors to lay me back down. I feared for my life, and I honestly believed that I was going to die. My mom was in the room with me. She too was afraid. She had tears in her eyes; she had never seen my body react that way. The experience was very traumatic for her, and she didn't know what to expect. After seeing the way my body responded, they laid me back down, left the room, and gave me some time to rest.

When the doctors returned to the room, they told me that they wanted me to try to sit up again. My previous experience made me afraid, and I didn't believe I could do it. As I struggled with the decision between either lying down or trying to sit up again, I made the decision to give it another try. I knew that fear could keep me from making it to the next stage in my process, which was rehabilitation. I finally overcame my fear of sitting up and gave it another try. To my surprise, my body responded entirely differently. My symptoms lessened, and I didn't faint. At that moment, I realized that my fear had been greater than the actual obstacle.

Once I was sitting up, the doctors asked me if I would like to attempt my first transfer from bed to wheelchair. With assistance, I did so successfully. Pushing through the physical barriers to being comfortable while sitting up and learning how to transfer was the beginning of my journey to adjusting to life in a wheelchair.

Conquering fear was imperative for my growth. I soon realized that fear lived in my mind and had a manipulating force over my body. Had I not overcome the fear in my mind, it would have prevented my body from pushing through the physical barriers that I was once afraid to overcome.

It is imperative that we don't become content just because we've seen an improvement in our circumstances. Sometimes we take pride in any light that comes our way after we've seen the darkest days. However, we can't allow a little light to keep us from experiencing the sunshine. Continue to grow; challenge the limitations that we impose mentally. The pain required to get better must not serve as a barrier to healing and progression.

Fear should not govern us. We must conquer it in our minds to reach the next level. No matter what we experience mentally, physically, or emotionally, be optimistic and confident that we have the ability to change our circumstances. Willingness to overcome must be stronger than fear of the pain. Challenge fear by pushing through the thoughts and feelings of your painful experiences. Regardless of what we've been through, please know that life is purposeful.

Nothing you have experienced is in vain. Focus on the bigger picture, which is the positive impact that you will have on this world. Remember that small tasks accumulate as you reach larger goals. Don't overwhelm yourself by trying to move too quickly.

Daily Shift

As you move forward in the process, overcome fear by implementing the following daily shifts:

1. Don't allow fear to make you accept an uncomfortable situation.
2. Challenge your fear by courageously reducing the power of your past experiences.
3. Don't be intimidated by the pain you must endure in order to get better.
4. Focus on your willingness to win.

Affirmation of Courage

I am courageous.
My mind is free.
My soul is free.
Fear does not live inside of me.
I refuse to be governed by fear.
My willingness to win is much stronger than my fear of defeat.
I am a conqueror.

ESCAPING HATRED

Hate is too great a burden to bear.
—Martin Luther King Jr.

Although I was racially profiled and shot by the Pittsburgh police, I had to make a conscious decision not to be consumed by the negativity that racial division brought to the forefront of my situation. About three months had passed since I was shot. And it was tough for me to combat all the negativity surrounding my case. The media developed fictitious and one-sided reports long before I was given an opportunity to defend myself.

The obvious facts of my case were ignored in efforts to incriminate me. I was lied about by the officers involved and blamed by officials who were protecting the system. The media portrayed me negatively. Many viewers were very critical of the falsified reports.

Their comments included racial slurs and death wishes. I tried my best not to watch or read anything that would provoke negative thoughts, but I regularly browsed the Web for hours, reading racist comments about myself.

I wanted to avoid the negativity, but I found myself drawn to those articles. It was hard to ignore articles and reports highlighted day after day in the media. With every story, I felt myself become saturated with hatred. I felt as if the negativity was inescapable. The more I focused and fed myself with negativity, the stronger the magnetic pull of hatred had on me.

The commentary on my case ignited hatred and negativity within me that I'd never experienced before. I found myself consumed by the racial tension that created the great division between blacks and whites in my city.

It was tough being singled out because of the color of my skin. I sat and watched the assassination of my character while the officers received no repercussions for being overzealous and violating conduct policies. The intelligent, peaceful, loving, and charismatic person I was before I was shot was diminishing right in front of me. I became consumed by the negativity, baffled by the lies, and angered by the pain.

Imagine being thrown into a fiery pit of hatred, consumed by negativity that changed the core principles and beliefs of who you were. How do you get out? How do you stay true to your core principles and beliefs when you are consumed by everything that goes against them?

To do so, you must create a barrier that serves as a force field of positivity. I began to surround myself with positive mentors. I read empowering literature that focused more on human development than racial division. I also watched motivational videos to help me redirect my focus from all the media negativity.

The videos I watched and the books I read included messages about the power of thought, the power of faith, and the importance of a positive mind. These messages helped me become optimistic; instead of being consumed by anger, I found myself speaking life to my situation. I found hope in the very things I once deemed hopeless.

You must create a barrier to separate yourself from the negative happenings in your life. This barrier serves as a buffer from the consuming contents of your fiery pit. As you neutralize the pit of negativity that intends to destroy you, you will find strength to climb out.

During this period, there was much that I couldn't control, and I allowed it to consume me. But there came a time when I had a paradigm shift that caused me to focus on the things that I could control, like my core beliefs, my attitude, my thoughts, and my perspective about my circumstances. When you understand what you have control over, you must make a conscious decision not to be self-destructive.

When you find yourself surrounded by negativity, you must redirect your focus to positive things. You must not allow negativity to consume you, or you will remain negative. It is imperative that you find positivity to nurture your spirit so that you become productive in the midst of adversity.

You can't control what happens to you in life, but you can determine if it will consume you. It's up to you to redirect your energy toward positivity instead of negativity. In any situation, you can change your attitude, your perspective, and your beliefs. Be optimistic!

Daily Shifts

As you go throughout your day, escape hatred by implementing the following daily shifts:

1. Create positive barriers, protecting you from negative thoughts, emotions, and actions.
2. Separate yourself from negative energy.
3. Focus on things you can control.
4. Stay positive in the midst of adversity.

Affirmation to Overcome Hatred

The weight of hatred is cumbersome.
I will not be shackled by its chains.
Although I cannot control what I am faced with,
I will control my response.
God has given me strength to combat any force.
I will not be overtaken.
I will not be consumed.
I will recover.
I will prevail.
I will win this battle against hatred.

TRANSFORMATION

> And he who searches our hearts knows the mind of the
> Spirit, because the Spirit intercedes for God's people in
> accordance with the will of God.
>
> —*Romans 8:27*

Being shot five times and nearly losing my life as well as my ability
to walk left me with an immense amount of hatred. The hatred I felt
toward the police officers was so overbearing that it hurt my heart.
I was angry and bitter, I felt defeated and I was full of rage. I was
unforgiving.

The hatred was so overbearing that my spirit rejected it, and, as a
result, it lived in my mind but never entered my heart. My spirit
protected my heart, which ultimately prevented me from inflicting
more pain on others and myself. Allowing this amount of hatred to
enter my heart would have changed my character. I would have been
a very negative person, fueled by hatred, which would have led to
adverse acts.

The hatred in my mind was so strong that it nearly saturated my
life. I was advised by loved ones to begin praying to help combat
the hatred I felt, but I honestly didn't know how to pray. I'd never
received any instructions, and I had never prayed before.

I didn't grow up in church, I didn't consider myself religious, I didn't
know any scriptures, and I felt like my relationship with God wasn't
worthy of prayer. But I didn't realize that I didn't need to speak the
words that were in my heart. God could see the words that were in
my heart before they made their way out of my mouth.

The prayer in my heart was so powerful that it transformed the
hatred in my mind. As I continued praying, I began to notice that
the hatred in my mind abated. I thought less about the people who

hurt me and focused more on what I could do to make things better. No longer was my heart in conflict with my mind, and I felt peace.

This transformation was ultimately responsible for the renewal of my character, because my negative thoughts transitioned into positive thoughts. My negative words progressed into words of positivity. And as a result, my actions became pure. I became optimistic, and my transformative light dominated the darkness in my life.

I now understand that even though I didn't have a personal relationship with God, I was still worthy of prayer. Open communication with God is available to everyone, and it doesn't have to be formal. Through my experience, I have realized that the prayer in my heart was stronger than any negative emotions that entered my mind.

You must open your heart and allow God to wrap your heart in prayer. You can open your heart by simply being receptive to the goodness within you. The goodness within you will connect you directly with a higher power and immerse you in peace. You will know you've opened your heart when you feel a wave of unexplainable faith overtake you, regardless of your circumstances. Praying with your mind has the potential to lead to egotistical, opinionated, and ultimately emotionally driven prayers. What we desire in our minds can contradict what we yearn for in our hearts.

Daily Shift

As you go throughout your day, accept your transformation by implementing the following daily shifts:

1. Open your heart by focusing on love and positivity instead of allowing yourself to be consumed by your negative emotions.
2. Make use of the open line of communication you have with God.
3. Embrace your positive transformation.
4. Allow your transformative light to guide you to a positive life-style.

Prayer of Transformation

Dear Lord,
I come to you with an open heart.
I seek understanding.
I know that there are negative people and things trying to bring me
down.
But I know that you are stronger.
Transform me into your light.
I am ready to be transformed.
My heart is open.
I release myself of all negative emotions.
Even when I can't find the words to say, God,
you listen to the prayers of my heart.
My heart is wrapped in prayer.
My mind is strong.
I speak life, not death.
I am pure.

Amen.

OWNING YOUR ADVERSITY

You must discover the strength that's within you in order to overcome the adversity around you.

When I was in the hospital, people would call and tell me that they would come by and see me. I looked forward to visiting hours, but some days hours would pass by when those I was expecting to show up didn't.

I can remember being angry; it was a terrible reality that everyone around me seemed to be going on with life as usual while mine was at a complete standstill. I can recall browsing through social media, observing many of my friends as they went through their days, looking happy. I was angry that they were having fun and conducting life as usual without me.

I was in a state of depression, dealing with an astronomical amount of pain, but my friends were enjoying life. I was hurt, bitter, and, honestly, jealous that I was the only one in such great pain. Just as we'd all experienced good times together— I wanted us to experience pain together. I wanted them to hurt, and I wanted them to experience sleepless nights. Honestly, I wanted their lives to come to a complete standstill, just as mine had. I didn't want to push through the pain alone. Unfortunately, it took me a while to realize that it was my adversity, not theirs.

Once I realized that they had lives of their own and that they had no obligation to stop what they were doing to appease me, I then began to understand that it was selfish of me to desire that they put their lives on hold because of the pain I was experiencing.

I understood the harsh reality that some people were moving on, enjoying their lives, as they were entitled to. Others stayed away simply because my pain was too hard for them to bear, and I respected their process. As time went on, I gained understanding and realized that to overcome adversity I had to first push through my negative thoughts.

Next, I had to release people from the emotional obligation associated with my pain and selfishness. Initially, I wanted their lives to stop because mine had. I knew that wasn't possible, but, selfishly, I did not care, because my thoughts were filtered through my pain. The pain caused me to place unrealistic expectations on people, which left me disappointed and made my process harder than it had to be.

Once I released others from my unrealistic expectations, I became more grateful for the support offered to me. Releasing others from unrealistic expectations made me embrace my process while acknowledging my God-given strength.

Although I was grateful to have a strong support system, discovering my strength and ability to push through the pain and get through tough moments was essential. I learned through my process that unrealistic expectations were a direct result of my attachment to people; I wanted them to cater to my needs without considering them.

I expected others to put me first, even if it meant neglecting their process. I wanted these individuals to see me without understanding that they had lives of their own. I didn't care if they had to call off work, skip school, or cancel any other obligations. I just knew that I wanted visitors.

This was selfish of me, and it was an unrealistic expectation that I had to release to find peace in my process. I've learned to release myself of unrealistic expectations by simply being understanding of someone else's process and not feeling obligated to receive assistance. While all support was accepted and appreciated, lack of the support at the level I wanted didn't negate the love that I knew existed.

What you're going through may be extremely painful, and you may not know how to get through it on your own. However, it is imperative that you don't become a burden to those who are there to help you because you refuse to accept support in the way they chose to provide it. Pain has a way of creating an unrealistic desire for the people around you to respond to your needs in ways that exceed their capabilities.

Unrealistic expectations will ultimately push people away and cause you more pain. Instead of expecting people to always be there, learn to be grateful when they are. Placing obligations on those around you distracts you from the blessing of them being there. Be careful not to place physical demands on your emotional needs. Don't allow the anger and frustration of your process cause you to inflict unnecessary pain on your loved ones.

You must release people of the emotional obligations associated with your pain and selfish thoughts. Expecting someone's life to stop because of your current circumstances isn't possible. No matter how extreme your circumstances may be, life must go on for you and those around you. Mandating unrealistic expectations from those around you prolongs your healing. Once you release people of unrealistic expectations, you will have a peace of mind, leaving room for gratitude in the midst of the pain you are experiencing.

Daily Shift

As you go throughout your day, you must take ownership of your adversities by implementing the following daily shifts:

1. You must release others of their responsibility to push through your pain.
2. You must release others of unrealistic expectations.
3. Show gratitude for the help given to you.
4. Take ownership of your process.
5. Discover your own strengths and abilities to push through the pain.

Affirmation of Accountability

Even in my weakest moments I have strength.
In times of confusion I seek understanding.
I will cleanse myself of excuses.
I refuse to drown in adversity.
I will lift myself up.
I will hold myself accountable.
I will discover my own strengths and abilities.
I will push through the pain.

SPIRITUAL AWAKENING

My brokenness is an asset to who God has created me to be.

Losing my ability to walk was one of the most devastating occurrences in my life. In the beginning, it didn't seem real; there was nothing I wanted more other than to walk again. I thought about it all day, every day. The thought replayed in my mind no matter what I was doing.

When I was around family and friends, I couldn't enjoy their company because the presence of my pain overshadowed the love that filled the room. I couldn't experience the joys of fatherhood and the milestones that my son was reaching because I was overly consumed by my pain.

I recall the moment that my son began to take his first steps, I couldn't help but think about what it would be like once I started taking steps of my own. I couldn't even enjoy a simple movie because my mind was overtaken by thoughts of never walking again. The constant reminders of never being able to walk again dominated every single moment of my life. In the midst of repetitious thoughts about walking again, I was told over and over it was impossible.

Every time I was told that I would not walk, another piece of hope was taken away from me. My desire was so great that the reality of never walking again made me reach a suicidal state. I contemplated overdosing on medication, causing physical pain to both myself and others.

I had somehow convinced myself that my entire existence was reduced to my ability to walk. I came extremely close to allowing my physical desires to sabotage my spiritual purpose. I was in a very desolate place, and I felt like without the ability to walk I had nothing.

My happiness seemed dependent on my ability to walk. I was at my lowest point, and I couldn't see beyond my physical brokenness. But something happened that caused my spiritual awakening. It was this moment that a light bulb went off and revealed to me how every experience in my life was connected.

The spiritual awakening showed me that a higher power was guiding me throughout my entire life. As I reflected on my life I learned more about whom I was as a spiritual being, where I was going and I also became more aware of all of my lived experiences. I was able to look beyond my physicality and view my life on a deeper level. God's vision for my life became clear to me, and my spiritual purpose became greater than my physical desire to walk again.

My spiritual purpose came with far more than my physical desires could provide. It came along with happiness from within, and it gave my life substance and meaning. It validated that I was here for something far greater than I could imagine. It showed me that my brokenness could serve as one of the greatest assets to my purpose if I viewed it from a spiritual perspective.

Viewing my life from a spiritual perspective brought peace and serenity and allowed me to enjoy each moment I was alive without being consumed by my circumstances.

Spending time with my son became more joyful because my spiritual perspective afforded me the opportunity to live in the moment without thinking about the pain I was experiencing. I was able to think about my blessings, and I felt blessed to have the opportunity to spend time with my family. I cherished the positive times more than I dwelled on my painful experiences. That was a true paradigm shift.

We all have things that we greatly desire, but we must focus on the things that God desires for us. Focusing on our physical desires brings a temporary sense of happiness, while our spiritual purpose renders life and peace. As I begin to concentrate on the things God had for me,

I began to understand the significance of my life on a deeper level. This discovery was the beginning of my spiritual awakening.

We must understand that the spiritual realm is what activates the physical realm. We are more effective physically when we are submissive spiritually. Our physical desires usually pertain to what benefits the self, but our spiritual desires can become an asset to the world around us. We all have physical desires, and God doesn't overlook the sincerity of our desires, but He makes sure that His will is fulfilled. God will only bless you with your physical desire if it enhances your spiritual purpose.

I have absolute faith that God will grant my physical desire and allow me to walk again at the appropriate time. I am patiently waiting for the fulfillment of my physical desire because I know that God's timing is perfect timing. God is giving me time to grow into my spiritual purpose. I am still seeking understanding of who God is, the works that he performs, and the purpose He has for my life. I know without a doubt that God has my desire in mind, and he will manifest it when it serves as an enhancement to my spiritual purpose.

Daily Shifts

As you pursue the things you desire in life, allow yourself to become open to your spiritual purpose by implementing the following daily shifts:

1. View your adversity from a spiritual perspective. Ask yourself, What is the Creator's vision for my life? And how will the Creator use my pain to help others?
2. Redirect your thoughts so that your spiritual purpose takes precedence over your physical desires.
3. Embrace the process of growing into your spiritual purpose.
4. Trust God's timing

Affirmation of the Spiritual Purpose

I am led by the spirit.
My spiritual purpose is greater than my physical desires.
I will not allow physical brokenness to break my spirit.
I will view my brokenness from a spiritual perspective.
My brokenness is an asset.
My mind will not be consumed with negativity.
I will not let my physical desires sabotage my spiritual purpose.
God is giving me time to grow.
I will embrace the process.
I will trust God's timing.
God will bless me with my physical desires.
My physical desires will enhance my spiritual purpose.
My spiritual purpose is in alignment with the will of God.
I am blessed.

PUSH YOURSELF

Being stuck in discomfort is more painful than pushing through it.

I arrived at rehab nearly two months after being shot. I weighed less than one hundred pounds, and I was extremely fragile. I struggled with simple everyday activities, but through rehab, I would regain some independence. This process was tough because I was learning how to care for myself all over again. When I first arrived, I struggled with sitting up. The doctors would strap me into a harness and lift me from my bed and place me into my wheelchair.

Every time I sat up in my wheelchair I became extremely dizzy and nauseated, and I would vomit on myself. This made it difficult for me to gain weight. I was on a strict nutritional diet that included lots of protein and lots of supplements. That process alone was difficult for me; there were days when I wanted to give up and lie back in the bed.

There were moments when I felt sorry for myself, and that made it even harder for me to push through. But there was no way I would get stronger if I didn't eliminate self-pity and push through the pain. The more weight I gained, the stronger I became.

When I first went to rehab, it was a struggle for me to lift less than five pounds. But I had to push through, and I worked my way up to lifting twenty-five pounds within weeks. I was in an extremely challenging and painful position, and I hated everything about my circumstances. However, I used my hate toward the situation as motivation to get me through it.

The process came with significant challenges, but I never gave up. As I got stronger, I began to function at a higher level of independence. Initially, someone took care of my every need: feeding, cathing, bowel training, and bathing. I had to discover new ways to independently care for myself so that I could go home. I no longer had function over my bowels and bladder—so finding new ways to complete those tasks independently was a top priority for me.

My doctors introduced me to options that they felt would be best in my physical condition. There were some options I wasn't willing to settle for, which meant that I asked more questions and explored new alternatives.

I made a decision to learn to catheterize myself and learn to complete my bowel training. These processes were tough, and I didn't thoroughly master them until after being released from rehab. Knowing that I wanted to be as independent as possible required that I push through the difficulties of scheduling bowel training and cathing myself four to six times daily.

The newness of the processes made me very nervous. I didn't accept the discomfort of my circumstances because I was focused on the end result: going home. The more I learned to care for myself, the closer I was to going home.

I looked forward to going home to be with my family and living life as independently as possible. Although I was excited, I didn't know what life with a spinal cord injury outside of the hospital would be like. I was extremely nervous.

The hospital was my comfort zone because it had everything I needed. But home did not. I wasn't sure how I would adapt. Since I wanted to be home more than I wanted to be in the hospital, I had to overcome the negative emotions associated with leaving my comfort zone. I began to notice that physical preparation alone wasn't enough; I had to start to prepare mentally. Therefore, I had to gain control over my thoughts, not allowing anxiety to prevent me from working as hard as possible so that I could finally be home with my family.

I eventually began to push myself. There wasn't a perfect time for me to go home, but by pushing myself, I made sure I was in the best shape possible to go home. Although I wasn't physically in perfect condition, mentally I was prepared for the push. When it was finally time for me to go home, I was extremely grateful.

My first day home was easier than I expected. I realized I wasn't as dependent on others as I'd thought. My parents were able to provide me with the care I needed to be comfortable at home. We always have what we need in our lowest moments. I held onto my family for support as I pushed through the pain. It is imperative to find something to hold on to while you're pushing. My family helped me push, so I wasn't doing it alone.

You must understand that you can't wait for the perfect conditions to start pushing. Even in your weakest moments, you have all the resources you need to push. There will be moments when you must push emotionally, mentally, physically, and spiritually. Pushing in one area will make up for what you may be lacking in another. When I was first injured I wasn't physically able to push. I had to push mentally until I gained the strength to push physically.

You won't always feel like pushing, and sometimes it's easier to feel sorry for yourself or quit. But where does that get you? Quitting makes everything harder by prolonging the painful process. Releasing yourself from self-pity gives you the power to take control over your life. Self-pity is taking advantage of what you cannot do instead of taking advantage of what you can. While taking advantage of what you can do, you may be faced with limitations.

Don't allow the limitations that you face to stop you from pushing. Find ways to work through your limitations by asking questions. Knowledge of your limitations gives you a clear understanding of what you need to do to get past them. Don't be discouraged when you encounter boundaries that force you to explore new options.

"A true champion can adapt to anything," said Floyd Mayweather Jr. Pushing yourself will require that you activate the champion inside of you so you can find the courage to leave your comfort zone. Being stuck in your discomfort is more painful than pushing through it. My will to go home was much stronger than my desire to be comfortable in the hospital. Don't allow your strong will to be reduced by contentment in your comfort zone.

Daily Shift

As you work to overcome life's greatest challenges, take ownership of your role in the process by implementing the following daily shifts:

1. Release yourself from self-pity.
2. Ask questions so that you have a clear understanding of what you are capable of.
3. Be ready to adapt.
4. Push with every ounce of energy that you have so you can get to where you want to be.

Affirmation of Push

I will push myself.
No matter how difficult,
I will push myself.
No matter how tiresome,
I am strong enough to withstand adversity.
Because my will is strong,
no boundaries will discourage me.
Because I am courageous,
I will push beyond my limitations.
I will break all barriers.
Because true champions adapt,
I will not wait for perfect conditions.
I will prepare myself mentally.
I will prepare myself emotionally.
I will prepare myself physically.
I will prepare myself spiritually.
I will eliminate self-pity.
I will ask tough questions.
I will continuously push.
Where I lack, my support system is backing me.
Where my support system is lacking,
God is backing me.
I have all the resources I need to push.
I am committed to pushing myself.

FALLING

It's not if you get up but when you get up.

During rehab, the therapist would lift me out of my wheelchair and sit me on the floor, and I would then have to get back into my wheelchair. Transferring into my wheelchair from the floor was tough, but it was necessary. It was inevitable that the time would come when I would fall, and I would have to find a way to get back up. I hated that difficult exercise, and I never believed that I would fall so it seemed pointless.

To my surprise, I fell at home late one night while attempting to make a transfer from my bed into my wheelchair. Transferring was— and still is a daily task for me. Typically, I accomplish this very easily and successfully. However, on that particular night I wasn't successful, and I ended up falling unexpectedly.

When I fell, I instantly became angry. I hated the officers who shot me because they were responsible for me being paralyzed. I hated my wheelchair, and I hated the fact that I had fallen. When I fell, I initially thought someone would come and help me. I called for help, but no one heard me. I was angry when no one answered my call for help.

At that moment I didn't consider that maybe no one was home or that they were asleep and couldn't hear me. I was just angry; I felt like someone should have been there to help me. I found myself just lying on the floor, angry and reluctant to get up. I spent nearly ten minutes on the floor, focusing only on how much I hated my position. Within that time I never attempted to get up. Instead, I proceeded to pull my covers off the bed and attempted to create comfort in the position I despised.

As I lay there in pain, I realized that I didn't want to be on the floor, but it was completely up to me to tap into my strength and get back up. I realized that my negative state of mind was keeping me in an undesirable position, so I decided to focus on getting up. Once I got up, I realized that falling out of my chair was symbolic of falling in life. This incident gave me a new perspective on my entire situation.

Getting shot was one of my lowest moments in life. I felt that there was absolutely no way I could get back up. I had been knocked down in various ways. I was unable to walk, my innocence was taken away from me, my teenage years were turned into chaos, and there didn't seem to be a realistic solution that would allow me to get back up.

The only practical solution at the time was for me to harvest hate against the officers who shot me and took my ability to walk. I hated them for the excruciating pain they caused me. I hated them because they took my independence away, and ultimately, I hated them for being the reason I fell so low in life.

Having fallen so low, I felt like my pain was unidentifiable to everyone around me. Being in that much pain left me unreceptive to help, and, as a result, I felt alone. No one could hear my cries from within, so no one could render assistance as I needed it. I was longing for someone to repair my spiritual brokenness, but people could only provide physical support.

I convinced myself that lying in pain would provide more comfort than if I decided to push through it. For nearly two years, I stayed on the metaphoric floor I fell on. I finally made a choice to get up. I realized that I couldn't allow my physical circumstances to inhibit my mental ability to get back up. Your state of mind after a physical fall determines the magnitude of the fall. Falling is inevitable, but getting back up is a choice.

It is nearly impossible to go through life without falling. Unexpected situations revolving around family, friends, finances, business, etcetera, will stand in as your metaphoric floor. You must prepare for these moments just as I did while in rehab. Preparation doesn't make falling easier, but it makes getting back up possible. There won't always be someone around to assist you to get back up; you must rely on your God-given strength to find ways to get up when life knocks you down.

People will offer you physical support, but that won't be enough to repair your spiritual brokenness. Sometimes we are unreceptive to physical support because our pain needs spiritual attention. The lack of spiritual support will cause you to feel alone. Being alone after falling is one of life's greatest teaching moments.

After my fall, I discovered that I could courageously rise above my pain by utilizing the power and strength that God had given me. Lying on the metaphoric floor of life caused me to waste a significant amount of time trying to figure out how to make the floor more comfortable rather just getting up.

Far too often we find ourselves in compromising positions much longer than we have to because of our desire to seek help. You must make a conscious decision to get back up when life knocks you down. Your life experiences have prepared you for your fall. Your perception of your position will either discourage you or motivate you.

Daily Shift

As you navigate your way through the unexpected falls of life, you can get back up by implementing the following daily shifts:

1. Don't get comfortable on the floor.
2. Allow past experiences to serve as preparation.
3. Courageously rise above your pain by utilizing the power and strength that God has given you.
4. Make a conscious decision to get back up.

An Overcomer's Affirmation

It's not if I fall, but when I fall.
It's not if I get up, but when I get up.
I will get up with dignity.
I will get up with power.
I will get up with courage.
God has given me strength to rise.
Adversity has given me opportunity to inspire.
I will not lie in sorrow.
I will give all glory to God.
And I will overcome.

FIGHTING FOR LIFE

Only a man who knows what it is like to be defeated can reach down to the bottom of his soul and come up with the extra ounce of power it takes to win when the match is even.

—Muhammad Ali

When I reflect on my life before being shot and paralyzed, I view my life as that of a typical teenager. Life was great. I was surrounded by good people and good energy. I didn't have a care in the world. I had recently graduated from high school, and I was perfecting my craft as a boxer. I woke each morning and hit the track. I understood that one of the key elements in boxing was endurance. Running became a part of my daily lifestyle. Before I did anything else, I ran. I also spent countless hours training for amateur fights in hopes of being a professional boxer one day.

I shadowboxed for hours to prepare my muscles for the real fight. Although I spent a lot of time shadowboxing, sparring was by far my favorite thing to do. Sparring is an actual fight between you and your opponent. My trainer would always tell me, "The key to fighting is to hit but not get hit. But if you do get hit, even if you are knocked down, get back up and fight harder than you've ever fought before." Boxing taught me about the discipline of both the body and mind. Running five miles was physically exhausting, but I wouldn't allow myself to quit mentally. As a result, I completed each workout.

I understood early on that physical preparation alone wasn't enough; the mental capacity to deal with hardship was also essential. At the age of nineteen, I wasn't entirely sure who I wanted to be, but I knew that I was destined for greatness. Life was good, my future was bright, and possibilities were endless. I now know that the principles I learned inside the boxing ring were preparing me for the fight of my life.

After being shot I literally fought for my life. Now, I was fighting to have a regular life, which involved more than physical recovery. It was a mental, emotional, and spiritual fight. This fight for my life was the ultimate knockdown, but it didn't classify as a knockout because I refused to allow my physical circumstances to diminish my mental capabilities.

The pain of being knocked down wasn't great enough to overshadow my purpose. There were moments when I didn't know if I would live or die, but I kept fighting because I knew there was a purpose for my life.

There was no way that God allowed me to live without a purpose. It was in the most painful season of my life that God began to minister to me. I was always a fighter, but in those moments of pain, God revealed to me what to fight for. Sometimes it's easier to shut down when life becomes too painful, but we jeopardize our purpose when we refuse to push through adversities. As long as you push through the pain, you will be able to tap into your purpose. Your purpose can be used positively to impact thousands, and possibly millions, of lives.

Daily Shift

As you go throughout your day, operate in your purpose by implementing the following daily shifts:

1. Think positively by focusing on your purpose, rather than your pain.
2. Embrace your pain and use it as a tool to help you stay grounded in your purpose.
3. Take back your power from the pain by fighting through your toughest moments. It is then that you will find peace among your greatest adversities.

Affirmation of Purpose

I will push through the pain.
I will tap into my purpose.
I will not be defeated by adversity.
I will find peace in the pain.
I will pull power from my pain.
I will push through the pain to find my purpose.

PAINFUL PURPOSE

When you connect the pain to your purpose, you gain control over your destiny.

For about a year after I was shot, I was in a very deep state of depression. No matter how strong my support system was, I always felt alone. Life was gloomy, and it seemed almost impossible to find any joy within. I still smiled; however, deep down inside I was hurting.

All that I wanted was for someone to recognize the depth of my pain without me physically speaking. I had people to talk to about my pain, but depression took over and silenced any support that was rendered.

After spending so much time being depressed, I somehow found comfort in my state of misery. I didn't have any confidence in myself or my future. I was uncertain of the direction of my life and didn't believe that life in my new circumstances had a purpose.

The wheelchair limited the avenues I had thought would lead to my success. My state of mind was pessimistic, and I experienced moments when I didn't want to live. Although I didn't see any potential or positive possibilities regarding my future, people around me still believed in me. Somehow they knew my tragedy hadn't limited my purpose.

My physical condition and emotions became completely overwhelming, and I had an emotional breakdown. I remember a moment at my grandma's house one day when I felt completely helpless, defined by my wheelchair. I recall telling my grandma that I didn't want to live anymore and that my life didn't have purpose.

My grandmother didn't allow my situation to limit her perspective on the assignment that God trusted me to fulfill. Although I wasn't able to tap into my spiritual purpose, my grandmother began to speak to my purpose. She understood the power of communicating with my purpose instead of my pain. She told me, "Grandson, you are great, and your life still has purpose. One day you are going to change lives all over the world. You are going to be a source of inspiration to young people all over the world." As she spoke life into me, I experienced chills throughout my body. I realized that I had to use my voice to change the world.

My grandmother reminded me that the weight of my God-given assignment would enhance my spiritual purpose. She didn't believe that my pain was in vain. She knew that the pain of my process would be an asset to my purpose. My grandmother believed in me when I didn't believe in myself.

Her belief in me was so strong that it made me believe in myself. I began to internalize the positive words and energy she had given me. Her encouraging words were what I needed at that moment. They helped me focus on the positive aspects and possibilities of my life instead of focusing on all the negatives.

In your low moments, God knows the people you will be receptive to, and He will speak to you through those individuals. It may be a loved one, a child, or even a complete stranger. Keep in mind that God will also speak to you through things around you, perhaps a movie, music, or interactions with others. No matter how much pain you're experiencing; allow your spirit to remain open so that you can become receptive to your calling. Receptivity allows you to see the purpose in your pain.

There is a difference between understanding the process and going through the process with understanding. Going through the process with understanding allows you to experience pain knowing you can pull purpose from it. Experiencing pain without acknowledging the purpose gives too much power to a temporary moment. But when you connect the pain with your purpose, it gives you power over your destiny.

Daily Shift

As you go through your painful process, remember to tap into your spiritual purpose by implementing the following daily shifts:

1. Surround yourself with people who will speak to your purpose in the midst of your pain.
2. No matter how painful, remember that your God-given assignment will enhance your spiritual purpose.
3. Pull purpose from your pain.
4. Allow your pain to serve to enhance your purpose.

Affirmation of Purpose

I will communicate with my purpose.
I will pull purpose from my pain.
I will not allow my pain to control my destiny.
No matter how painful my assignment,
I will not give up.
I will stay faithful.
I will be inspired.
I will stay strong throughout the process.
I trust that God will allow my pain to enhance my purpose.
I trust that God will speak life into me by using the influences around me.
God believes in me even when I do not believe in myself.

LIFE EXPERIENCES

You must look beyond the oppression in adversity and see the opportunities in it.

I was once a young man who didn't care to educate myself through reading. Schoolwork wasn't difficult for me; I had the ability to excel, but I didn't feel it was expected of me to excel. I felt like a statistic before I was given a chance to work against it. Even with the odds stacked against me, I managed to graduate from high school. The education system didn't seem to cater to me as a young black male in a positive light. It was more widely accepted for me to engage in negative activities than it was for me to advance academically.

I recall doing research projects on Michael Jordan, Allen Iverson, Jay Z, and Tupac, all of whom were in the entertainment business. I was encouraged to do research projects on these individuals, which led me to believe that entertaining was the only way I could be successful. My dreams of working in the entertainment industry seemed intangible when my teachers informed me that it was nearly impossible.

I wanted to perform in front of thousands of people like Jay Z, or change lives, like Tupac Shakur, and my teacher laughed and told me that I should pick up a trade instead because I was good with my hands. Although her suggestion may have come from love, it was very discouraging and deterred me from furthering my education. Until I learned to educate myself, I separated myself from the limitations others placed on me.

To educate myself, I began to learn about many leaders, including Malcolm x, Stokely Carmichael, Ella Baker, August Wilson, Rosa Parks, George Jackson, Harry Belafonte, Bob Moses, Nelson Mandela, and a host of others who inspired me to stand up for justice. Through educating myself, I discovered there were opportunities beyond the adversity I would face.

Acknowledging that my life was purposeful beyond the limitations that others placed on me gave me the opportunity to visualize myself as a leader. I found purpose in my pain, which led me to my vision. I knew that I wanted to stand up for what was right, but I wasn't sure where to start. So I used every painful situation I'd experienced in my life as a pathway to lead me to my ultimate purpose.

Everything I thought could break me became the very things that gave me something to fight for, helping me to evolve into a great leader. My negative experiences as a student in a public school system molded me into a student advocate and mentor. My experience being shot by a police officer empowered me to become an activist. Now I use my voice to stand up against police brutality and systemic racism.

Life is our greatest teacher. It renders lessons that we can gain only through our own experiences. My most powerful leadership assets, including my strength based mindset, positive attitude, high expectations regardless of my circumstances, and integrity, come from lessons I learned during my most painful circumstances.

Once I discovered my leadership qualities, I used other resources to inspire me to employ my negative experiences as building blocks toward great leadership. One of the most powerful resources I utilized was history. Learning about historical leaders I could relate to gave me a blueprint for who I could become, even with all the adversities I faced. These leaders gave me a foundation for visualizing who I would become and how my painful experiences could enhance my legacy.

Visualizing myself as a great leader made me look at my life experiences from a different perspective. Viewing the bigger picture of my life and the legacy I wanted to create helped me to pull the positives out of every negative situation. Once you push through the pain, you take back the power from every negative experience that once had power over you. My negative experience in school no longer served as a barrier but as a tool for constructing success.

As you go through the process of becoming the person God has purposed you to be, you must embrace but not be consumed by the limitations other people may place on you. Limitations can be opportunities when you change your perspective and view them as enhancements to your purpose.

Be strong in the face of limitations others place on you; as you overcome them you will build your legacy, making those who came before you proud and giving those coming after you strength. Knowing who you are and what you are up against is necessary for your journey. Seek knowledge of self and embrace the fullness of your being.

Remember that education is not confined to the walls of a building. Education is limitless, and with it you can break any barriers. Acknowledge that your life is purposeful beyond the limiting barriers that others place on you, and visualize yourself as the leader you were born to be. Use your pain as a tool to find your purpose. Adversity is always an opportunity to tap into and enhance your purpose. You can enhance your purpose by taking control of your life.

Every obstacle intended to slow you down, harm you, or take you away from God's purpose for your life can be used to help you grow into your purpose. Your most painful experiences can be used to develop you. View your life beyond the oppression and adversity with optimism, and you will see the opportunities at your fingertips.

"If you change the things you look at, the things you look at change"(Anonymous). You must view even your negative experiences as building blocks for your purpose. You can pull teaching moments from even your most painful experiences. These teaching moments are God's gift to you that you must utilize to change lives, starting with yours.

Daily Shift

As you go through the process of evolving into the person God has created you to be, capitalize on every life experience by implementing the following daily shifts:

1. Understand that life is your greatest teacher.
2. Use negative experiences as teaching moments.
3. Don't define yourself by limiting barriers that others have placed on you.
4. Visualize yourself beyond your circumstances.

Embracing your Experiences

I vow to learn from all of my life experiences,
No matter how painful,
No matter how dark.
I am not limited by my experiences.
My knowledge is not confined to the structural walls of a classroom.
I will educate myself.
I will push through the pain.
I will pull the positives out of every situation.
Negative moments are now teaching moments.
My vision is more powerful than my circumstances.
I am successful.
I am knowledgeable.
I am great.

INSECURITIES

Creating yourself is not being who you are but being who God created you to be.

I remember feeling like just another black boy who was shot by another white cop. Although I survived those unfortunate circumstances, I felt like just another statistic. I knew that I had a story, but I didn't understand the significance or the power of my story.

The pain of my circumstances prohibited me from seeing my purpose. I didn't have enough confidence to tell my story, and I honestly didn't know how. I stuttered when I spoke and sank deeper into my insecurities. I felt anxiety about who I was, and I felt anxiety about who I would become. I felt like my life was over. I didn't feel like there was anything I could do to become great. I'd always desired to make my parents proud, but I no longer felt I could.

I remember very vividly what it felt like when I received the news that a family member, Aaron Donald, was drafted to the NFL. My dad came in the house, excited about Aaron's accomplishments. He screamed with excitement, "Yo, dog, Lil Aaron got drafted to the NFL! I know Big Boom is happy as can be." Big Boom is Aaron's dad, and my father's excitement for my uncle and cousin left me feeling insecure regarding my physical state.

I was excited too, because I loved Aaron and knew that he had worked very hard to make it to the NFL. However, his accomplishments validated my insecurities and made me feel inadequate. I continued wondering how I would make my dad proud. The thought that I would never make my mother proud haunted me.

I began to wonder how I could make my own son proud. Because I was in a wheelchair, I felt like there was nothing I could do; my son would have no reason to look up to me. I didn't see anything dignified about being in a wheelchair. I felt like I would be a liability forever, rendering absolutely no assets. I felt reduced to the boundaries of my circumstances, which caused me to feel insecure and invaluable. I felt like my life had no meaning.

I hated the position I was in, but the only thing I could do to change it was to change it. I knew I could no longer sit around and do nothing. I had to pull myself together and make the necessary modifications. I began to embrace who I was, including my physical circumstances. I had to rely on my strong foundation for insight about what was still possible. A foundation built on faith was all I needed to become the person God created me to be.

When I had nothing left, I hoped that my possibilities were greater than my circumstances. At the time, I didn't physically pray, but God understood the prayers of my heart. I decided that I no longer wanted to feel inadequate. I was tired of feeling as if my life had no meaning. I started visualizing myself happy, living a productive life despite all I had been through.

The visualization gave me the motivation to take the proper steps to create myself. Visualizing who I would become provided hope against my insecurities. I began to understand that I had a story. Although I was another statistic, I was also a rare exception because I had survived. I knew I could be a leader; I could be a voice for those who had lost their lives. I began to see the boundaries of my circumstances as opportunities to create myself.

I used my social media platform to create the person I wanted to be. At the time, I was depressed, suicidal, insecure, unhappy, and pessimistic. But I didn't let those feelings stop me from becoming something greater. I began to describe myself as the person I wanted to be instead of the person I was. I started to change the things I said about myself in hope of becoming what I was speaking. I began saying that I was king, that I was great, strong, ambitious, and positive.

As I was making this transformation, some people closest to me called me a hypocrite because they didn't understand my growth; nor were they willing to accept it. I didn't allow their negative views of who I was distract me from the process of becoming who God created me to be.

I would post on social media to motivate and inspire others, even when I was feeling the complete opposite, which helped me combat my negative emotions. The positive feedback I received from providing inspiration despite how I was feeling inspired me to use my story to empower other people. I started receiving messages about how amazing I was and how strong I was, and I literally began to believe those descriptions were true.

I remember receiving messages from people on the verge of suicide. After visiting my page and seeing how I was dealing with my pain, they said I gave them strength to live. In this way, I started to discover my purpose.

I realized that my story wasn't about destruction but healing. There was more to my story than just being another police brutality statistic. But it was completely up to me to use it for God's intended purpose. While I used my story for the purpose God intended for me, he allowed others to help me heal. People didn't understand that their words were being used to heal my brokenness.

As their words began to heal me, I was able to see who I was beyond the pain. I didn't initially understand that God created me to be a leader. He created me to be great, and He created me to withstand the pain. But he was waiting for me to become exactly who He created me to be. As I began to realize this, I started working toward being everything I was designed to be.

A painful experience can be debilitating to your future if you don't discover the purpose in it. Circumstances can strip you of your confidence and your drive to become greater, but your life can still be purposeful. Often we allow our hardships and circumstances to define who we are, but we must become the change we wish to see and not the pain inflicted upon us. Becoming the change you want to see is doing the work God has called you to do.

Nothing that you have been through is in vain, and your pain is purposeful. God understands the magnitude of the pain you have endured. He will use unorthodox resources to help heal your brokenness. It can be difficult to view your adversity as purposeful, and you may find yourself comparing your purpose to the purpose of others. Do not worry about pleasing those around you; navigating in your purpose is dignifying and will be pleasing to God.

Everyone has a different process and a different assignment. Do not deem your God given assignment as inadequate because of your inability to understand its significance. Intentionally speak positivity in your life, and battle your insecurities by visualizing your future self. Create positive reminders of who you will soon become.

Think with the end in mind. Remember that God allowed you to endure the pain so you can become who He created you to be. Allow what you have gone through to help you become who God has created you to be. Creating yourself means embracing your process and accepting the challenges that come along with your change.

Daily Shift

As you embrace the process of creating yourself, implement the following daily shifts:

1. Visualize your future self and think with the end in mind.
2. Create positive reminders of who you are and who you will soon become.
3. Understand the significance of your process.
4. Aim to please God, not people.
5. Embrace your process, and accept all challenges that come along with your assignment.

Affirmation to Become

My adversity is meaningful.
My pain is useful.
My life is purposeful.
I am able to visualize who I am beyond my pain.
I am able to visualize who I am beyond my brokenness.
I will become the change I wish to see.
I will do the work that God has called me to do.
I do not intend to please man,
but I intend to please God.
I will embrace my process.
I will accept all challenges.
I will overcome adversity.
I will create myself.
Separation | 74

SEPARATION

The catalyst of growth is separation.

At one time, I was physically, spiritually, mentally, and emotionally depleted. I was in the process of healing, and I was also fighting for my freedom. At that time, I lacked confidence in every aspect. I felt like a burden when I was around other people, so I didn't feel comfortable around friends. The additional help I needed to get in and out of the car, needing to be carried upstairs, and several other things made me feel like a burden.

My lack of confidence was not limited to the physical but was also intellectual regarding my legal case. I sat and listened to my parents discuss my case with my lawyers, but I didn't have the confidence to use my voice. I didn't feel comfortable conveying my thoughts and asking certain questions.

I found myself sitting among family and friends, trapped inside my thoughts, silenced by low self-esteem. My independence had been stripped from me, and my entire life changed. Initially, it felt like the changes were for the worse. I was an entirely different person. Essentially, I felt like I was existing and everyone else around me was living.

I separated myself from what was going on around me-from the familiar. I didn't know then that that was a necessary step for a positive transition, because through that separation I could begin to discover a new passion and a new purpose.

I developed a passion for reading and watching informative videos, something I had never been interested in before. I began to become inspired, because the majority of the people I read about made an impact on the world at very young ages. Learning that greatness and influence didn't have an age attached, I realized that I didn't have to wait to activate my greatness.

My lack of confidence was what God used to allow me to separate myself from the familiar. During my separation, I discovered my passion, which led to my intellectual development and introduced me to my purpose.My lack of confidence separated me from people, but it brought me closer to my purpose.

Sometimes separating yourself from what's familiar helps you grow beyond the limitations that you have internalized as a result of your current circumstances. The catalyst to growth is separation.

In the moments when I separated and silenced myself from the outside world, I was able to hear God speak to me. He revealed my calling. I would be used as a vessel to change the world. At that moment, I didn't understand the magnitude of my calling, but I knew I was on the right path, and I knew that greatness was inside of me.

It can be easy to allow low self-esteem to make you believe that you are inadequate. But that isn't true. You were born to be great. You are great. God will isolate you from everyone around you so he can prepare you for your journey.

Often, we are consumed with worldly things that cause us to disconnect from the Creator. Physical, mental, and emotional separation provides space for you to reconnect with God. Connecting with God will give you strength to push through adversity, confidence in your blessings, and faith that you are protected by the mighty power of God. When God knows that you're ready, you will be called to fulfill your purpose. God placed me in this wheelchair for something beyond my imagination.

Daily Shift

Embrace the process of finding your purpose by implementing the following daily shifts:

1. Separate yourself from what's familiar.
2. Release the limitations you have internalized as a result of your circumstances.
3. Separate yourself from the outside world so you can discover your purpose.
4. Listen to God as He reveals your greatness.

Affirmation of Growth

I will separate myself from my comfort zone.
I will separate myself from the outside world.
I will not allow limitations to stunt my growth.
The catalyst of growth is separation.
I am committed to growing.
I will be led by the voice of God.
He will reveal my purpose.
I am destined for greatness.

SPEAK IT INTO EXISTENCE

Your life has purpose. Visualize your life beyond your current circumstances and speak great things into existence.

It was a year and a day after my shooting, and I was tired of feeling inadequate. I was tired of being weak. Tired of being run over by people. I was tired of worrying about going to prison. I was tired of being afraid of a corrupt system. I was tired of struggling with hopelessness. I was tired of my inner battle with faith and disparity. I was tired of mornings feeling like midnight. I felt like I was trapped in prison, accompanied by depression, anger, bitterness, and suicidal thoughts.

The walls were quickly closing in on me. I was tired of my light being dimmed by the adversities of life. I had already been through so much, including losing countless loved ones. My sister had been tragically killed when she was ten years old. Now I was dealing with the harsh reality of being shot and paralyzed at the age of nineteen. I felt like I couldn't take anymore. It seemed like a dark cloud of destruction followed me throughout my entire life. I was so overwhelmed with pain that there were days I didn't want to wake up. The pain felt inescapable.

I desperately longed to break out of the deep despair and emerge into a brighter future. It seemed nearly impossible—until November 12, 2013. That day, many people from the community came out to support me, hold local politicians accountable, and criticize the district attorney for filing charges against me and not the officers responsible for shooting me.

As I sat in front of the council members in a large room at Pittsburgh's City-County building, I made a life-changing proclamation about my life.

I never considered myself as a religious person, but at that moment God spoke to me. Not only was He speaking to me, He was also speaking through me. At that moment my spirit was revived through the words God had given me to speak.

I vividly remember nervously holding the microphone with a firm grip. I asked God to guide my words. The energy in the room was intense. I saw tears in the eyes of the mothers sitting behind me. I felt the anger and frustration of the fathers. I also felt the worry from my peers, who knew how easily they could fall victim to police brutality.

The members of city council looked at my supporters and me with blank stares. I wondered if they were at all concerned over the injustice I'd experienced. I wanted my voice to be heard. I spoke timidly. "I'm here because I was shot and paralyzed by the Pittsburgh police a year ago, and I want to make sure that doesn't happen to anyone else. This year has been hectic and it's been hard. There are days when I don't even want to wake up."

As I spoke, the spirit of God revealed to me that my words had power. With every word the atmosphere became more intense. My supporters wanted to take a stand. The body language of the city council members revealed that they were uncomfortable. "When I was shot, I had a choice to give up, but I refuse to give up. I'm in this chair, and I feel like I have a point to prove."

By the end of the speech, the spirit of God had taken full control over my words, allowing me to declare life-changing things that were far greater than my circumstances. "My future was bright before. I'm in this chair now, and I'm not going to let my future be dim. I'm going to make sure my future is brighter than ever. I'm going to shine. I'm going to make sure that everyone remembers me no matter what."

Those words let the leadership of the city know that I refused to be broken. I looked them directly in the eye; I meant what I said, and they knew it. I was not there for games. I was not there just to make a statement. I was there to let them know that I was about change and I was not afraid to stand up for justice. After making this proclamation, I felt completely free. I felt as if my spirit had burst free of bondage. For the first time since being shot, I was confident.

The light within me shined brighter than the dark cloud that had once hovered over my life. At the time, I didn't understand what was taking place in my spirit, but I knew it felt really good. I had no idea that the words God had given me to speak about my life would serve as a true declaration for my life.

Life experiences can make you feel spiritually and emotionally dead, even after you survive unforeseen occurrences with the ability to kill you. The pain can be so overwhelming that you feel stuck, hopeless, and depressed, exhausted and desperate for any relief. Don't seek physical healing for spiritual damage. Drugs, alcohol, shopping, gambling, and other temporary comforts can't provide the spiritual healing you're in need of. When you are feeling exhausted and desperate, seek God. He will revive your spirit.

Allow your spirit to be revived through the positive and encouraging words God gives you to speak about your life. Understand that your words have power to speak life and death. Therefore, you must allow God to speak to you and through you. Profess a life-changing proclamation about your life.

Remember that the words God gives you to speak are a true declaration of what He can do in your life. So speak great things about your life with confidence, and walk the path God has called you to. Your life has purpose. Visualize your life beyond your current circumstances, and speak great things into existence.

Daily Shifts

Begin to attract positivity into your life by implementing the following daily shifts:

1. Be mindful not to seek physical healing for spiritual brokenness.
2. Allow God to speak to you and through you.
3. Speak what you see until you see what you speak.
4. Be clear about what you want; write it down and act on it.
5. Proclaim your victory.

Affirmation of Faith

I have faith that God will turn my tragedy into achievement.
I know the pain I've experienced is purposeful because it could've been bereavement.
I am free of negativity.
God will cleanse my spirit and free me from mental captivity.
I refuse to give up.
God will give me strength so I cannot lose.
He will speak to me and through me.
I will speak what I see until I see what I speak.
My life is purposeful.
My future is bright, and my light will never dim.
I am victorious.

ACCEPTANCE

Going beyond your thoughts puts you in higher realm of faith because it surpasses where you are.

Three years later, the reality of being paralyzed is just as painful as it was the day I found out I would never walk again. In the beginning, I honestly thought that I would get better. To my surprise, I didn't get better physically, but when I learned to view my life from God's perspective, it activated my faith on a higher level. Throughout my life, I've experienced a great deal of pain.

Many times I asked God, "Why me? Am I strong enough? What's next?" Living life from my wheelchair is painful. I'm healthy but unable to walk. Every day is a struggle. Sometimes I'm depressed, angry, and full of hatred. There isn't a day that goes by when I don't desire to walk, but I realize it may never happen. My daily struggles exceed what the eye can see. I'm faced with adversity on many levels: physically, emotionally, and mentally.

I try my best to stay positive. I am a symbol of inspiration, but the reality is that the pain still exists. It hasn't subsided with time, but with faith I'm able to navigate beyond the emotions from the pain so I can understand why God has chosen that I be in this position. I know that God trusts me with adversity, and I can accept all that comes along with the weight of my process.

I refuse to allow my pain to withhold me from God's purpose for my life. Faith leads me through the process of pain, which transcends emotions to acceptance. It is imperative that I accept my God-given assignment and not allow the process to break me.

God knows that you are strong enough to withstand adversity without being broken. Not being broken doesn't equate to not being emotional. Emotions are a form of acknowledgment of the pain. To push through the pain, you must first acknowledge that it exists.

Once you acknowledge that the pain exists, you must work through your emotions, allowing your faith to govern your thoughts instead of your thoughts governing your faith. Faith doesn't see our situation for what is but sees it for what it will become. Therefore, faith teaches us how to deal with the pain. Once faith teaches you how to handle the pain, you develop an understanding of the responsibilities that come with your assignment. Understanding your assignment increases your tolerance of the pain, giving you strength to accept it.

Daily Shift

As you go through your day and navigate through your painful reality, embrace your assignment by implementing the following daily shifts:

1. Accept the reality of your pain and the weight of your assignment.
2. Know that your life has a purpose; everything you've been through is a puzzle piece to help you to fulfill your assignment.
3. View your life from God's perspective of you.
4. Trust the process.

Affirmation of Acceptance

I acknowledge that my pain is real.
I will endure the weight of my assignment.
God is using my adversity as a roadmap to my purpose.
I will stay the course.
I will not be broken.
I will not be overtaken by my emotions.
I understand the responsibilities of my assignment.
I embrace the lessons of my pain.
Through faith, I accept where I am.
Through faith, I accept where I'm going.

LEADERSHIP

Leadership resides in all of us, but we must be open to the opportunities that expose our leadership characteristics.

I've been a leader my entire life, but after I was shot I didn't know how to lead. I faced a great number of emotional challenges after being confined to a wheelchair, and my confidence was broken. Before getting shot, I was a popular kid. I was a ladies' man, physically fit. I drove the best cars and wore the latest fashions. I was leading from the outside, rather than the inside. My confidence was dependent on what surrounded me, but it didn't come from within.

My pain was so great that it prohibited me from looking within myself and acknowledging my true leadership potential. I focused on all that I lost before God introduced me to two powerful leaders who played strong roles in my development as a leader.

Brother Jason Rivers, a well-known community leader in the Pittsburgh area, identified with my pain and was inspired by my natural ability to lead. He invited me to speak to a group of young men. Among those young men were other leaders and school board officials. I felt out of place and unwanted, due to the controversy and politics surrounding my story.

Many didn't want to get involved. Keep in mind that I was shot during a time when the #BlackLivesMatter movement was not a trending topic. People cared, but they didn't know how to be involved without jeopardizing their livelihood and undergoing scrutiny from their peers and leaders. Brother Jason went against what was popular, accepted, and safe so he could help reactivate the leader inside of me.

I remember feeling nervous. I didn't know what to say to those young men. I didn't know if they would be receptive to my story. After all, we weren't in the same position. How could I capture their attention? I began sharing my story. I was honest about what I had been through, what I was currently going through, and the obstacles ahead of me.

The more I opened up, the more I observed the connection I had with the young men in the room, and I realized that my story was both impacting and inspiring to them. Speaking to the young men gave me a sense of relief. Sharing my story allowed me to pour out the pain that had been fermenting inside me. Their attentiveness and engagement confirmed that I wasn't alone.

Although no one else in the room shared my current position, we were all connected by painful experiences. At the conclusion of my speech I received a standing ovation, and at that moment I realized that I was of service to both myself and others. This experience gave me the opportunity to engage with other leaders who served as my personal mentors.

Brother Malcolm Thomas, another influential leader in my life, was a spiritual and wise individual, very positive. Brother Malcolm set the standard for me as a leader. His interactions with the community, his love and respect for people, and his thoughtfulness made him a great leader.

There is a quote that says, "Doing is never enough if you neglect being." He showed me the significance of "being" a leader who leads from the depths of the soul, not from the emotions of the moment. He believed that youth empowerment led to adult leadership. In every interaction with him, I felt empowered, and he influenced me to become a better leader.

Leadership resides in all of us, but we must be open to the opportunities that expose our leadership characteristics. Jason Rivers gave me an opportunity, but it was my receptivity that led me to the path of rediscovering the leader inside of me. Leadership requires a certain level of bravery.

When Jason Rivers challenged the status quo, he placed his commitment to leadership above his job description. His courage and willingness to navigate in faith connected me with my purpose, which changed my life and the lives of others. Being a leader isn't enough. To change lives, you must be led by the spirit.

Being spiritually led is significantly different from being emotionally led. You will find yourself in unfamiliar and unpopular places, but you must remember that God has placed you exactly where you are-with purpose.

Brother Malcolm was extremely purposeful in my life; his leadership and influence came at a time when I needed them most. He used every opportunity to empower me and also to offer a true example of what a leader is. You must embody leadership, and you must also remain teachable so that you can teach those around you. You must lead by example.

Daily Shift

When you discover that you, too, are a leader, embrace the positive characteristics of leadership by implementing the following daily shifts:

1. Remember that leadership comes from within.
2. Boldly navigate in faith when challenging the status quo.
3. Remain teachable.
4. Lead by example.

Affirmation of Leadership

From my personal mentor Malcolm Minnekhekh Thomas

We must give up to go up.
We must give up to grow up.
We must give up on the way up,
and give up even more, to stay up.
I cannot teach what I do not know.
I cannot lead where I will not go.
I am because we are.
We are because I am.
I am my brother's keeper.
I am my sister's keeper.
I am destined for greatness.
Because I attract what I am.

GREATNESS

> Greatness resides in each and every last one of us. We must
> not allow pain and hardship to suppress our greatness.

If you always rely on the greatness of others, it is impossible to discover your own greatness. After being unjustly shot, I faced up to twenty years in prison. So much had already been taken away from me. To add insult to injury, my freedom was also in jeopardy. But my greatness, my ability to fulfill my purpose and my legacy without compromise was mine. No one could take that from me.

I began to realize that even with all that I had lost in the process, my greatness was enough to give me the strength and confidence to fight for justice. I decided I would organize my very first rally. There were people around me who didn't think I could achieve that. The magnitude of the task made others believe that the help of popular organizations and traditional leadership was necessary for it to happen.

I didn't allow the insecurities of those around me to cause me to doubt my own greatness. I began utilizing all my resources. I used an unorthodox approach to gain the support of my community, spending countless hours visiting schools, barbershops, hair salons, malls, nightclubs, and community events.

That untraditional approach allowed me to tap into my greatness. In doing so, others were able to see their greatness as well. They began to understand that they also had a voice that could stand up against the injustice we were culturally conditioned to accept. I understood that my voice played a significant role in utilizing my greatness to challenge the status quo of traditional leadership.

At the time I was organizing my first rally, I didn't fit the traditional culture of greatness. I wasn't a part of a major organization; nor did

I have thousands of traditional supporters. But my voice and my influence in the community helped me to restructure the culture of greatness.

Greatness radiates from the inside out. Your values and purpose make you great. Many people were looking at my issues, and that prevented them from seeing my value, so they didn't think I qualified to be great. But I didn't need anyone to validate my greatness because I was navigating in my purpose.

Creating my own standard of greatness allowed me to successfully turn my pain into purpose. Throughout this process, I relied on my ancestors and their fight for justice. They didn't allow pain and hardship to suppress their greatness. Instead, they went against what was popular and common and fought for justice. Greatness didn't end with our ancestors; nor did the fight. I stood up against the cultural conditioning of injustice, and I relentlessly fought until I obtained my freedom.

My fight for freedom wasn't just against the police officers who shot me. It was also against systematic oppression we were culturally conditioned to accept. Society wanted me to believe that I had to sit back and let the system fight me, but instead, I took a stand and I fought back. I fought for myself; I fought for my freedom. I fought for my community and its safety. Ultimately, I fought for peace, love, and equality. And I continue to fight!

Throughout my process, I learned that tapping into your greatness requires that you do the exact opposite of what society expects you to do. People will tell you what you can't do, but you must rely on your greatness to tell you what you can do. You must utilize your greatness to stand up for yourself and others, which will ultimately lead to change.

Doing what is great is not always doing what is popular. You will sometimes be ridiculed for the cause and frowned upon for your bravery. Do not be intimidated by the status quo or you will never discover your own greatness. Don't allow your pain and hardship to suppress your greatness. You must tap into your greatness by operating in your purpose. Pursuing your purpose and doing what is right may cause you to be despised in the moment, but your greatness will live on forever.

Daily Shift

As you go throughout your day focus on the positives by implementing the following daily shifts:

1. Tap into your own greatness.
2. Don't be afraid to challenge the status quo.
3. Don't allow your pain and hardship to suppress your greatness.
4. Pursue your purpose, and do what is right.

Affirmation of Greatness

I refuse to be defined by this moment.
I acknowledge that I am great.
I am greater than any adversity.
I will overcome any obstacle that has been planted against my success.
I will operate in my purpose.
I will push through the pain.
I may be despised for the moment,
but my greatness will live forever.
I am great!

BEFORE BLACK LIVES MATTERED

> I survived the injustice of five bullets, but I was consistently shot down by influential leaders of my community, because assisting me was not the conventional thing to do at the time.

Imagine being shot by the police in an era before #BlackLivesMatter was trending. Imagine being surrounded by individuals who cared about injustice but were too afraid to take a stand. Imagine reading the mission statement of an organization that you felt could directly provide what you were in need of, only to find out that you were denied because of the politics, fear of losing funding, and lack of courage. Or, better yet, put yourself in my position. I felt like I was on an island full of community leaders who had the power and resources to help me, but they were either too afraid to help me or not willing to help at all.

I was in pain, experiencing one of the lowest moments in my life. The leaders who took pride in helping young black men such as myself were the same leaders who denied me access to services, love, and resources.

I needed help with coping, recovering and progressing, but many leaders and organizations were apprehensive about getting acquainted with me and my story because of the controversy surrounding my circumstances. I survived the injustice of five bullets, but I was consistently shot down by influential leaders of my community because it wasn't the conventional thing to do at the time.

During a great deal of my process, I felt bitterness toward those organizations because of the way they treated me. Once the #BlackLivesMatter movement became a trend, organizations and community leaders became more receptive to the movement. I began to realize that people support what's popular before supporting what matters. I was angry that people were using the trend for self-gain and not for change.

My pain existed before the hashtag gained popularity so I grew apprehensive about supporting the sensationalized #BlackLivesMatter Movement. When it's no longer trending in the media, victims' pain still exists. I felt like many local and national leaders were riding on the backs of victims for publicity, profiting from our pain without direct experience with that pain. I distanced myself from traditional leaders. I felt they were more connected to what had taken place in the past and were somehow removed from the current fight for justice.

I was forced to become my own leader. I realized that my God-given mission for my life was more purposeful than any mission statement I had read. I also realized that God hadn't allowed them to help me because he was developing me into one of His servants. Where those organizations were lacking, God allowed me to lead. I was searching for ways to cope, recover, and move forward, and God showed me exactly how to do that, despite being denied assistance.

I am spirit-led in every aspect of my life, and it doesn't allow me to get caught up in commercial fights for justice. Led by the spirit, I have learned to bridge the gap between the commercialized movement and the grassroots movement. As experienced leaders, we must know when to detach ourselves from our emotions so we can be effective.

Throughout my process, I separated myself from the emotionalism of my circumstances so I could become an effective leader. That doesn't negate the fact that I was experiencing pain and felt negatively toward leadership, but it helped me to be wise in addressing my feelings concerning my negative experiences with leadership.

I now use my experience to bridge the gap, rather than completely destroy the bridge between those directly experiencing pain and those who are indirectly experiencing pain. Bridging the gap affords me the opportunity to help leadership on both sides become more effective in their journey to change the world. I understand that an individual or one group cannot fix all the issues we are faced with in the world. It takes a collaborative effort.

Collaborative effort is impossible if we allow our emotions and negative experiences to dictate our leadership and prevent us from collaborating. Therefore, it is important that we put the ultimate goal before our feelings in order to make the best choices possible for the movement.

In life, you will experience moments of pain that leave you feeling angry, hopeless, fearful, and desperate. These moments can be classified as more than traumatic; you must use them as teaching moments from God.

During such teaching moments, you must silence the outside world so that you don't become consumed by negativity, which has the power to derail you from your God-given assignment. Negative emotions can cause you to become consumed by the chaotic circumstances. Therefore, don't allow your life to be governed by your emotions but instead by the spirit.

Do not allow yourself to become emotionally attached to temporary circumstances that are only a part of your process, and not your destination. Once you understand that rejection is temporary, you will also understand that rejection is necessary. In my experience, I needed the people who rejected me to develop as a leader. You, too, will experience painful rejections, but that experience will only strengthen you for your purpose. Knowing that all things work together for your good, be grateful for the experiences you may consider negative.

Daily Shift

As you began to turn your painful trials into powerful testimonies, you must discover the hero inside you by implementing the following daily shifts:

1. Take control of your own life by leading where others lack.
2. You are entitled to your feelings, but be wise in your approach when addressing them.
3. Whenever you're feeling low, trust God and pray, so that you can be spirit-led.
4. Embrace your rejections so that you can develop from them.

A Hero's Affirmation

I have experienced pain,
but the spirit has led me to peace.
I am led by the spirit to be the change I wish to see.
I will not focus on hatred,
because the spirit lies within me.
I have all the resources I need to save myself.
I will turn my fear into focus.
I am not afraid.
I am powerful.
I am invincible.
I am a hero.

GIVE UP TO GO UP

You must give up on the way up, and give up even more to stay up.

—Brother Malcolm Minnekhekh Thomas

Late one Sunday evening, I was thinking about the fact that I faced up to twenty years in prison, although I was the victim. I knew I had to do something or else my story would be swept under the rug, without national attention. Ultimately, I would be thrown in prison, like thousands of other young black men. In my desperation to be heard and to receive justice, I reached out to many national leaders. Only one answered my cry for help. Benjamin Crump, a lawyer, is well known for his role in the fight for justice for Trayvon Martin and his family.

After witnessing his impact on one of the most well-known cases of our time through the media, I felt it was necessary for him to assist in my fight for justice. I decided to contact him through the mainstream social media outlet Twitter. To my surprise, he contacted me within hours. My family and I were incredibly grateful and excited for the opportunity to receive the help we so desperately needed with my case. In our first conversation, he showed his eagerness to help. Within the next couple of days he was in Pittsburgh, ready to fight for justice.

Before working with Benjamin Crump, I didn't receive much support from the traditional Pittsburgh leadership. The traditional leaders are the gatekeepers, the ones involved with large organizations and politics. They have more contacts than an average citizen. Crump was able to help me to gain support from these individuals, who hadn't been publicly supportive before.

Initially, my family and I were skeptical of that support from traditional leaders. We weren't sure if they supported my case because they believed I was innocent or because of my affiliation with Benjamin Crump. However, I realized that I needed as much help as I could get to increase my chances of receiving justice.

Benjamin Crump worked to make my story a national story. He is known as one of the top civil rights lawyers, and my story immediately resonated with the racial tension involving other cases.

Although a white police officer shot me, I didn't want to be known as the black boy shot by a white officer. I wanted them to know that I was an intelligent young man who had a bright future ahead of me that was taken away when I was unjustly shot five times by the Pittsburgh police. I wanted them to know that society had failed me. I was taught to trust police officers, but the people I was taught to trust were the same people who caused my family and me astronomical amounts of pain.

I wanted my story to be known so it could bring the nation together to understand the significance of all lives, without racial tension or controversy. I did not want to cause racial division, which doesn't negate the fact that the shooting was racially charged. I wanted my story to provide solutions, not perpetuate the cycle of hatred and division.

I was incredibly grateful for all that Benjamin Crump did to help my story receive national attention and also for the supporters he attracted—but I realized that I needed more than just a national story. I was facing twenty years in prison and recognition wasn't enough to free me of the charges filed against me.

I began to understand that I could utilize my resources so that my story could be heard and also use those same resources in my fight for justice. I decided to release him from his duties as one of my lawyers, and I put more emphasis on my platform and my fight for justice.

I utilized my voice and made my story relate to all people. I spoke to the hearts of people instead of using their anger to fight a broken system. The spirit directed me to use my pain for a greater purpose. By not committing to any organization, I kept full ownership of my story. I could build bridges through courageous conversations about race and humanity without fueling racial tension and creating controversy.

Throughout this experience, I learned that it's important to reach out for help when you're in need. I didn't allow those who didn't want to help me to keep me from those who did. Some didn't support me initially, but I didn't allow skepticism and pride to keep me from embracing support when it was offered.

The support and assistance from others helped to build me up, giving me a larger platform and greater resources to share my story. I reached the point where God was leading me to utilize my voice; He had given me all the resources I needed for my story to be heard. I was called to make a tough decision, to give up to go up, and that's what I did. I had to release Attorney Crump, his platform, and his services. It was necessary so I could utilize my voice and my platform. In doing so, I not only shared my story, but I also helped to develop solutions and try to prevent others from experiencing the pain I have experienced- or worse.

In life, sometimes people you expect will help you won't respond to your cries, but don't give up. If you need help, keep seeking help. God will send the right people to assist you at the appropriate time. Not all assistance will be a permanent. Learn when to release people from their duties so they don't hinder your greater purpose. Remember that you must give up to go up.

Daily Shift

While working to improve your circumstances, learn to utilize the resources around you and the power within you by implementing the following daily shifts:

1. Remember that God will send you the help you need when it will be most beneficial to you.
2. Don't allow pride to prevent you from seeking help.
3. Don't allow help to become a hindrance to your purpose.
4. Remember that some people are part of your process but not part of your destiny.
5. Take control of your God-given platform.

Affirmation

I am destined for greatness.
I have a God-given purpose.
I trust that God will provide me with all the resources
I need to fulfill my purpose.
I understand that not all resources will last forever.
Some resources are part of the process but not part of my destiny.
I will not allow anything to weigh me down,
For I must give up in order to go up.

FORGIVENESS

Do not repay evil with evil or insult with insult. On the contrary, repay evil with blessing, because to this you were called so that you may inherit a blessing.

—1 Peter 3:9

I am often seen as a man who is humble, strong, powerful, courageous, and one is who is full of hope, faith, and love. Most importantly, people see the God in me. However, I still struggle with many things. Forgiveness happens to be one of my greatest struggles. People equate my smile, positive spirit, and happiness with being forgiving. However, the reality is that I was unjustly shot five times by an overzealous police officer, someone society told me to love, someone society told me to respect—someone society said would protect me.

I know exactly what it's like to lay on a cold concrete street in a puddle of warm blood, my body riddled with bullets, gasping for air, and not knowing if I was experiencing my final moments on earth. I know exactly what it's like to have officers stand over my nearly lifeless body, hoping and wishing I would die.

Can you imagine the heartbreak, how afraid I was, not knowing if I would ever get a chance to meet my son or see the rest of my family ever again? I was faced with the fear of spending nearly the rest of my life in a cold and lonely cell for crimes I didn't commit. And although I am extremely faithful, my reality is that the doctors say I will never walk again. No, I haven't been able to forgive the officers for what they put me through. My life is completely different. I'm confined to a wheelchair, and I can't do many of the things I was once able to do.

The pain from what the officers did to me makes it tough for me to forgive them. Many elements related to me being in a wheelchair are invisible. The painful reminders are constant. People can only see the surface of my pain, causing them to believe that forgiveness is also surface. Although my pain runs deep, I am led by the spirit, which allows me to react contrary to the negative emotions I feel. I can view my life from my blessings instead of viewing my life from my pain.

Continued suffering is a result of our views, and changing the way I view things has caused what I view to change. I realize that I am not experiencing pain alone; my pain gives me a larger platform to help relieve others of their suffering.

I do have negative feelings toward the officers who shot me, and the system as a whole but I understand that to prevent it from happening to others, I have to redirect those feelings. I am dedicated to being a bridge builder, informing people about what happened to me and the pain I am experiencing. I encourage people to become the change we need in order to live in a peaceful society. I have developed a program called The Voices Project that enables individuals from the community to express their pain through a positive outlet and to connect with others who are experiencing pain.

Making pain purposeful allows you to be a blessing to yourself and those around you. Without making pain purposeful, you may focus solely on negativity, which has the ability to change your character and takes away from being a good person. It also takes away your power to heal the world that has harmed you.

Understanding my assignment and my purpose is the first step toward forgiveness. I know that God has trusted me with the task of repaying an evil with a blessing. Even after being shot five times, left paralyzed, wrongfully charged, and enduring pain on many different levels, I know that my assignment is to respond courageously with power, strength, faith, and love.

Although I made a choice to respond in a positive way, I understand that forgiveness is a process. And I'm willing to embrace the process of forgiving by acting in my purpose.

Even after experiencing the excruciating pain associated with being shot and the emotional turmoil from what took place that night and the aftermath of being wrongfully charged, I am still able to navigate in my purpose by being a blessing. I can look beyond the apology I never received, the lies formulated against me, and the spiritual wickedness that is continuously done to harm me. I am focused on my God-given assignment and my blessings, all while coping with the pain.

Society tells us to react to pain with an eye-for-an-eye mentality. But the spirit instructs us to respond by being a blessing. Instead of taking an eye for an eye, heal the eye when they take an eye. Inflicting pain on others cannot treat the reactionary cycle of pain; being a blessing despite the pain can only heal it. Your pain is real and your emotions are justified, but your actions don't have to align with your feelings.

Negative emotions will only increase the pain for both yourself and others. Forgiveness happens from the inside out, not the outside in. Healing starts from within, although you may still be under attack from the outside while you're healing on the inside. Once you start healing internally, you become less vulnerable externally.

The internal blessings create a positive atmosphere externally. Being a blessing creates a positive environment that is contagious to those around you, which will decrease the pain for yourself and others. So we must not focus entirely on the proclamation of forgiveness but on the actions of being a blessing. Focusing on the declaration of forgiveness alone may cause you to become more consumed with your pain. Focusing on being a blessing will lead you closer to forgiveness.

Daily Shift

As you navigate through pain, become committed to the actions of being a blessing by implementing the following daily shifts:

1.View your life from your blessings instead of viewing your life from your pain.
2.Turn your negative emotions into positive actions.
3. Remember that healing starts from within.
4. Realize that your assignment is not based on the actions of your offender.
5. Lastly, forgiveness is an action word; your actions outweigh your proclamation.

Prayer for Forgiveness

Dear God,
I come to you full of pain, with an unforgiving heart toward those who have harmed me.
But I understand that you are the God of love, grace, and forgiveness.
Grant me your love, grace, and forgiveness so that I may grant others the same as I journey through healing.
I come to you seeking understanding of my purpose and my assignment.
My load is heavy; I'm asking for strength so that I may carry it gracefully.
I ask that you turn my negative emotions into positive actions so that I may continue to do your will.
I ask that you cleanse my spirit, renew my mindset, and endow me with your peace.
I ask for a tender heart so that I may one day forgive as you have forgiven me.

Amen.

REVENGE

Revenge is taking power out of God's hands and putting it into your own.

Although I was unjustly shot five times by an officer and I do have feelings and opinions toward law enforcement, I haven't allowed my negative feelings to become resentment toward all officers. My emotional battle is constant. I encounter officers who are open to change, receptive to having dialog, and promoting peace between the community and law enforcement.

Sometimes I meet officers who seem to be racist and unfair, and they perpetuate the cycle of division between the community and law enforcement. It is very discouraging when I encounter such officers because it is a reminder of the night I was shot, and it ignites hatred within me. When I hear about developing cases involving police shootings, I instantly feel an overwhelming sense of hopelessness. I find myself in a battle between despair and hope. In that fight, I try my best to not to be overtaken by despair.

I don't allow myself to watch gruesome videos of young black men and women brutally beaten and murdered by law enforcement. I am very intentional about not being consumed by all the negativity in the world. Therefore, I control my thoughts by being intentional about what I allow in my spirit. I refuse to allow the hatred of the world to enter my heart, and I don't allow it to consume my mind. I have learned that being surrounded by negativity has the power to change my character if I allow it. It's tough for me to be positive without adding God into the equation.

Adding God into my equation serves as a paradigm shift, allowing me to view my circumstances from a spiritual perspective. I will never understand why providing my driver's license, insurance card, and registration weren't enough for the officers to stop accusing me of being someone else. I will never understand why I was unjustly shot. I will never understand why I faced up to twenty years in prison.

My spiritual perspective gives me a better understanding of my process as it relates to fulfilling my purpose. I use my purpose as the driving force to help me move forward. However, some people around me have negative feelings, thoughts, and emotions toward law enforcement because of what happened to me.

Even though I have embraced my process of healing, it is still very challenging for many of those around me. My parents are incredibly grateful that I survived, and they are very proud that I am changing millions of lives around the world with the work I do. However, their gratitude for and pride in the man I have become don't negate the pain that comes along with the trauma that the police officers inflicted upon my family and me.

I still see the pain and the heartache in my mother's eyes every time someone has to carry me up the stairs to get into her house. I wasn't born with a disability, and she understands that if not for the negligence of the police officers, I would be able to walk up her steps with no problem. I still see the frustration and the anger in my father whenever he looks at me, knowing that the officers caused his baby boy an astronomical amount of pain while he has to sit back and do nothing. My understanding that I have purpose and the process necessary to fulfill it doesn't eliminate the fact that I still battle anger, frustration, and depression.

The battle within is constant even as I go through my purpose-driven process with understanding. My knowledge regarding my process doesn't take away the pain I am experiencing. I don't desire revenge, but I do want justice. I don't believe in the eye-for-an-eye mentality. "If it's an eye for an eye, we will all end up blind." (Mahatma Gandhi) People have a misconception that because I was unjustly shot by an officer and because I deal with an enormous amount of pain that I feel a level of satisfaction when an officer is shot and killed. But I don't. I feel for their families. I don't want anyone to suffer.

I understand the reality of pain after losing something of such great significance. I'm a leader, and I'm an advocate for change and healing, not the continuous cycle of suffering. I can't call myself a leader if I want someone else to experience pain at the same level I have experienced, no matter what they have caused. There is a substantial difference between revenge and justice.

Justice is about seeking the moral principle of just conduct; revenge seeks to inflict injury in return for injury. Justice is about being hopeful and having faith that God will make things right. Justice comes from the heart, not the mind. If justice comes from the mind, then it becomes vindictive and resentful. Justice comes from the spirit because it supports what is right. Revenge is influenced by resentful and vindictive thoughts. Therefore, revenge means taking the battle out of God's hands and placing it into your own.

It is imperative that you view your circumstances from a spiritual perspective. Your spiritual perspective will give you a better understanding of your process as it relates to fulfilling your purpose. You can view your life from a spiritual perspective by adding God to your life to bring peace and understanding. You will still face the challenges of the trauma associated with what caused you pain because your purpose-driven process is a continuous battle.

Understand that the pain you are experiencing is necessary for your purpose. God is using it to develop you. Don't allow thoughts and emotions to move you to take matters into your hands. Revenge doesn't bring you peace.

You can take revenge but remain lost and hurt. Revenge is a perpetual cycle of pain and trauma that nobody wins. Inflicting pain on someone else doesn't reduce your pain. In fact, it can increase your pain because revenge places you in a worse position. That's because revenge means taking it out of God's hand and putting it into your own.

Revenge removes the focus from God and places it on who has caused you pain. Focusing on who has caused your pain instead of God prolongs your healing process.

We must look to God for comfort and not seek revenge from within. To receive true justice against the spiritual wickedness that has caused you pain, you must trust God and His ability to bring peace and healing and to restore balance. That is justice!

Daily Shift

As you work through painful circumstances, implement the following daily shifts:

1. View your circumstances from a spiritual perspective.
2. Seek God to gain a better understanding of your purpose amid pain.
3. Understand the difference between justice and revenge.
4. Remember that God's timing is perfect timing; you will receive justice in his perfect timing.
5. Trust God and his ability to bring peace, healing, and balance.

Affirmation of Justice

I will not seek vengeance.
I will not be consumed by hatred.
I will view my circumstances from a spiritual perspective.
I will trust God.
I will use my spiritual purpose as a driving force to stay motivated.
I will embrace my process.
My spirit is pure.
I will not be vindictive.
I will look to God for comfort.
I will look to God for peace.
I will not seek revenge.
I seek God.
I seek peace.
I seek healing.
I seek justice.
I trust that God will give me justice.

DISTORTED VISION

Always stay receptive to the information given to you, but know yourself and stay true to yourself so that your vision is not distorted.

Tapping into my purpose introduced me to a whole new world of possibilities that included many great people. As I began to navigate in my purpose, I became a household name, which brought a large population of supporters and more mentors. I was extremely excited and eager to take on any new venture. I began surrounding myself with great people who were full of fantastic ideas. They saw my greatness, and they started providing me with information they felt would help me capitalize from my greatness.

As I began to take in information and explore new ideas, I was involved in many different ventures that ultimately distorted my vision. As Les Brown, a motivational speaker, would say, I became the jack of all trades and the master of none. Involvement in many different ventures made it hard for me to focus on one thing at a time and distracted me from mastering one. I constantly started new things, but somewhere along the way they would fizzle out, leaving another possibility incomplete.

Starting projects without completing them generated critical feedback from my immediate circle, leaving me frustrated. My frustration over the truth regarding my habit of starting but not completing things caused me to shut down and left me unproductive.

I was on my way back to a depressed state because I began to question my purpose. I lacked clarity, and I didn't know what I wanted to do with my life.

For a time I found myself back in the routine of doing the things that others thought I should do instead of doing what I had been purposed to do. I was living out someone else's vision for my life, not the vision God had given me. I felt completely drained, and my spirit was letting me know I was doing the wrong thing.

The absence of clear vision claimed a significant amount of energy and left me drowning in possibilities that pulled me further away from my vision. Some of the ideas presented to me matched the things I saw for myself, but I knew it wasn't the right time.

It's important to take the necessary steps for achieving goals, but we don't have to reach the goal in the time frame others decide. I was trying to figure out what I wanted for myself while listening to what others wanted for me. I began to take notice that my vision for my life was distorted by what people saw in me that weren't governed by my purpose or what I saw in myself.

Most of those people had good intentions, but they were unintentionally placing limitations on me and my purpose. While the intentions of many around me were good, they weren't necessarily good for my vision or for what God had planned for my life. I begin to recognize that my vision was benefiting others more than it was benefiting my God-given purpose. So I completely shut everything down. I stopped watching TV. I didn't answer my phone, and I stopped using social media. I cut off all forms of communication, which enabled me to be led by the spirit. The spirit redirected me to my purpose. I spent a lot of time in silence, reflecting on my life.

I turned down the volume in my life so that I could tune into what I was purposed to do. This meant eliminating people, ideas, and ventures that weren't benefiting my vision.

Shutting down brought me closer to God, and the time I spent with God brought me closer to my vision. I then became more comfortable navigating in my purpose. I utilized my open line of communication with God. I had a very unorthodox approach to strengthening my relationship with God. It wasn't through church or religious groups;

it was simply freeing my space, time, and spirit so that He could interject his plans and purpose into my life.

During that time, I began to receive more clarity concerning my vision. I became more conscious of the ways I was spending my time and also where I was spending it. This consciousness created awareness and a spiritual navigation for operating in my purpose. Ultimately, I regained focus on my vision for my life, and I begin to see significant changes in my productivity. Most importantly, I felt happy and fulfilled in my purpose.

It is very easy for your vision to become distorted by well-meaning outside influences. It is entirely up to you to stay grounded in your purpose by utilizing your open line of communication with God. You must be receptive to those who understand the vision God has given you because they will let you know when you're off track. But not everyone will be receptive to your vision, which may cause you to feel rejected and frustrated.

Frustration is a part of the process, but you must not allow it to pull you away from your vision. Once you discover that you're working on someone else's vision and not the vision that God has purposed for your life, you must turn down the volume of outside noise and focus on what the spirit of God is telling you.

Understand that your purpose is in direct correlation with what God wants for you. He will give you all the resources you need to fulfill your purpose. Some resources and people are useful for the process but not intended for the destination. Know when you have used them for what God intended them for and let go gracefully. Being unreceptive to the thoughts of others doesn't discredit their value, but it does protect your vision.

Daily Shift

As you redirect your focus to the vision that God has given you, implement the following daily shifts:

1. Stay grounded in your vision by using your open line of communication with God.
2. Turn down the volume on outside noise and focus on what the spirit of God is telling you.
3. Discern what resources are good for your vision.
4. Understand that resources have an expiration date and may only be good for an allotted time.

Affirmation of Vision

God has given me a vision.
My vision will lead me to my purpose.
I will do what I am purposed to do.
I will not be overwhelmed by ideas.
I will not be overwhelmed by time lines.
Nor will I be overwhelmed by the expectations of others.
I am led by the spirit.
The spirit of God will lead me.
The spirit of God will keep me in good company.
God's timing is perfect timing.
I will navigate in my purpose,
for God has given me a vision.

PREPARATION

When you go through the process with understanding, you gain foresight. You know that every frustration, setback, and barrier is just preparation for the result.

While preparing to walk again, I was constantly reminded of the likelihood I'd never walk. It was extremely painful to face such a daunting reality, but I never gave up hope. Although I had no mobility and very limited feeling in my legs, I never let go of the hope that walking was possible. The doctors based their prognosis solely on medical research. However, my faith concerning my condition lay within the hands of God. No matter how many times I heard that I would never walk again, I never lost faith that it was possible.

My desperation to walk again did not cause me to give up; it led me to ask more questions and try different things. Every time I heard it wasn't possible, I relied solely on what was possible through faith. I remained emotionally attached to the pain of losing my ability to walk, but I used my emotions as motivating factors to continue trying.

The first time I inquired about RGO braces or reciprocating gait orthosis, which is a medical device used in therapy to assist individuals suffering from paralysis with walking, the doctor told me it was impossible. Due to my extreme weakness and level of injury that impaired my balance, I was told no. I knew there wasn't anything I could do about my injury level, but there was something I could do about my balance.

Attempting to improve my balance, I removed the tippers from my wheelchair that prevented me from falling backward and the arm rails that prevented me from falling from side to side. Removing the protective barriers challenged me to sit upright and balance myself in my wheelchair throughout daily activities. Both my mom and dad were worried for my safety. I fell regularly.

Once I could balance better, I faced yet another obstacle that was preventing me from getting leg braces. I'd acquired a bed sore while hospitalized that not only prevented me from getting braces but prevented me from going to rehab as well. The healing process took approximately three years.

For three years I had to use a wound vacuum, which is a device that prevented the wound from becoming infected. A nurse came three times a week to clean the wound and apply the wound vac to the bed sore. During the process of healing the wound, I watched videos online about how others with a T5 injury used RGO braces. Watching the videos kept me motivated; I believed I would be able to use RGO braces soon.

Unfortunately, the wound wouldn't close after using the wound vac alone. I had to undergo surgery. I was bedridden for three months after surgery, which was a painful reminder of my circumstances. I was reminded that I wouldn't be in my current position had they never shot me, which brought my anger toward the police to the forefront. I experienced a great deal of depression, but I knew that to receive the braces and become more independent, the recovery was necessary.

After I healed, I inquired about the braces again. I was told that it was possible, but another barrier prevented me from getting them. I was required to pay off a medical expense first.

When I was informed of my new responsibilities, I did what was necessary to pay off my medical expenses in hopes of finally receiving my braces. But, to my surprise, there was more. I then had to receive a prescription for rehab, a prescription for the braces, and clearance from my insurance company to fill the prescriptions.

Although I experienced many obstacles, I never let go of my vision of walking again. Instead, I understood that everything I had to overcome was part of the process. I knew I wouldn't be able to use the braces until I completed my process. I had an idea of how long it would take me to get the braces, but the process was much longer than I expected. Each time I was faced with an obstacle, I didn't view it as a setback. I used it as an opportunity to prepare for what was ahead.

After years of being told no, of enduring setbacks, of waiting and preparing, I finally received my RGO leg braces. When I went to rehab, my therapists were completely shocked. I knew how to get in and out of the braces. I knew how to both stand and sit in the braces.

The best part was that I knew how to walk using the braces. My therapists were both amazed and confused at how well I used the braces for the first time. They didn't understand how I had so much endurance and strength. They asked me how I knew how to use the braces. My response: "Preparation!"

No matter how many times the doctors told me I would not walk again, not even with braces, I remained faithful to what I believed and to the process. Even when faced with painful and emotionally draining obstacles, I continued to find hope. I understood the significance of the process because I went through the process with understanding.

My vision of walking again helped me to better understand what I needed to do to make it possible. Each time I faced an obstacle, my vision motivated me to push even harder to make my vision my reality. Without knowing where I wanted to be, I wouldn't have used the rejection I received as motivation to dig deep. In this case, rejection empowered me to push through the pain making my vision come true.

You must hold on to your vision tightly, even when you have nothing tangible to hold on to. Your vision will sometimes be all you have to keep you motivated and moving forward. Do not be intimidated by obstacles; understand that they are part of the process. Do not be discouraged when things do not go according to your plan; trust God's plan, and he will use every negative experience to empower you.

There is a significant difference between understanding the process and going through the process with understanding. When you go through the process with understanding, you have foresight. You know that every frustration, setback, and barrier is just preparation for the result. Your faith in the result must be so strong that the process cannot break you.

Daily Shift

As you go through the preparation process and encounter unforeseen occurrences, continue to be faithful to your process by implementing the following daily shifts:

1. Don't allow circumstances to prevent you from having what's yours.
2. Hold on to your vision when you have nothing tangible to hold on to.
3. Remember that what seems permanent now is not always permanent.
4. Have faith in your vision and prepare for it.

Affirmation of Preparation

Through faith all things are possible.
There will be obstacles;
there will be setbacks.
But I will go through the process with understanding.
Everything I endure will strengthen me.
My vision will keep me motivated.
I am strong.
I am faithful.
I am prepared.
The process cannot break me.
My faith is unbreakable.

FINDING GOD

Find the courage to share your story of finding God because you may be able to help others to strengthen their relationship with Him.

I am often asked what religion I practice. I don't practice any particular religion. However, I do believe in God. My life experiences have caused me to disengage from traditional religious practices. I was never interested in church. I didn't know how to pray, and I had no desire to read the Bible.

I view myself as a spiritual being having a human experience. Throughout my journey, I have been invited to church. I have also been encouraged to read scriptures, but that hasn't increased my desire to engage in traditional religious practices.

My lack of engagement has caused me to ask myself why. Why don't I like church? How come I don't pray traditional prayers? Why don't I have the desire to pick up the Bible and read?

Through introspection and trauma, I found the answers buried deep inside of my soul. I discovered that almost every experience I had with religion, dating back to early childhood, was negative.

My first encounter with church was when I attended my older cousin's funeral; he lost his life to gun violence. Growing up, I lost many loved ones: friends, people from my neighborhood, and close relatives, including my little sister. My early exposure to death made me associate my feelings about religion and church with funerals. Gospel music, the Bible, and even the smell of church reminded me of death. When I did attend a regular church service, I felt like an outcast because I didn't know church etiquette.

I always felt like church people were very critical of outsiders, even though they, too, had sinned. However, despite my negative experiences with church and religion, I established a relationship with God at a young age. I was around religious people, but I was never forced to conform to their religious beliefs. That freedom provided me with an opportunity to find God on my own. I remember attending Bible studies. I felt bad because I didn't like reading the Bible. My mom always reminded me, "It's not about the religion. It's about the relationship." Gaining an understanding of the significance of having a relationship with God taught me to trust God at an early age. I established this relationship with God, even though I didn't attend church or read the bible.

When I found myself in a deep pit of pain, God revealed Himself to me. It wasn't religion, and it wasn't about eloquent prayers or the ability to quote scriptures. It was the presence of God in the midst of so much pain. There was a sense of warmth, love, and care that wouldn't allow me to harvest hate because His presence was so strong. I had felt that presence before, but this time I was conscious of communication with a higher being, and I was receptive.

Through all the pain, I became more sensitive to how my spirit was communicating with the spirit of God. What began as a gut feeling became an actual conversation with God.

The more I communicated with God in an untraditional way, the more He revealed to me. God knew what I was receptive to. Through this experience, I embraced the uniqueness of my circumstances instead of looking for God to reach me in the way He has reached others. I now understand that we are all different, which means that we are all receptive to different things. God in His infinite wisdom understands each of us and our individual needs. Throughout my journey, God has spoken to me in many different ways, through various religious backgrounds and through many things I experience daily.

The spirit leads me, and my spirit is sensitive as I communicate with God. I must remain open, because I never know who or what He will use to reach me. I am now open to reading the Bible, Quran, or any other religious book. I am also open to visiting Churches, Mosques, or Synagogues because I understand what was preventing me from engaging in traditional religious practices.

I am completely comfortable with my spirituality. I never know where God will call me to hear His message. Because I understand the power of a relationship with God, Allah, the Creator, Jehovah, Yahweh, Jesus, or whomever you refer to, I can fully utilize my open line of communication. My open line of communication helps me to stay grounded in my divine purpose. It brings me peace, it helps me to stay positive, and it allows me to go through my process with understanding.

God will find you exactly where you are. He will be sensitive to what you need, because He understands all of your life experiences. It is your responsibility to be open-minded and receptive to the voice of God. This voice will speak directly to your spirit. When you have strong feelings about something, listen carefully as He reveals Himself to you. God will reveal your purpose, and He will help you find peace in the midst of adversity.

Do not become discouraged if you receive judgment from those who don't understand you. God loves you just as you are and will use your painful experiences and the things that you may be ashamed of as tools to bring you closer to Him. Be receptive, and utilize your open line of communication with God. Don't allow negative experiences to discourage you from seeking God. Find the courage to share your story of finding God; you may be able to help others strengthen their relationship with Him.

Daily Shift

As you work to build a stronger and more meaningful relationship with God, implement the following daily shifts:

1. Be open-minded and receptive to the voice of God.
2. Remember that God will find you exactly where you are.
3. Utilize your open line of communication with God.
4. Build a strong relationship with God.
5. Embrace your spirituality.

Prayer of Presence

Dear Lord,
I know that I am not here for myself or by myself,
for I know that you are here with me and I have been called to
serve you.
I trust that you will meet me exactly where I am.
As I go through this journey, I desire to strengthen our relationship.
I am not perfect. I understand that no one is perfect, but I ask that
you open my heart and mind so that I may be receptive to your will
for my life.
If I am not walking the path you want me to walk, I ask that you
reveal yourself to me so that I will align myself with your purpose
for my life.
I know that everyone has different life experiences, but you
understand our uniqueness.
I trust that you will use my unique life experiences to help me walk
in my purpose.
I realize that I will be judged by others, but God, you are the
ultimate judge.
Therefore, I want you to know that although I may fall short in the
eyes of man,
I do love you, I do serve you, and I do fully commit myself to you.

Amen.

ARMOR OF GOD

10. Finally, be strong in the Lord and his mighty power.
11. Put on the full armor of God, so that you can take your stand against the devil's schemes.

Ephesians 6:10–11

I often talk about faith and what it means to be faithful, but there are times when it's difficult to be faithful when you lack a spiritual perspective about your circumstances. When much is taken away from you, the losses make it challenging to appreciate what you have left. For an extended period, I believed that my life had a purpose, but I didn't fully understand my calling or the significance of my process. I lacked faith in my purpose, even though I believed that God had a purpose for my life. I just couldn't seem to understand why I survived.

I had been extremely close to death— but I managed to survive the trauma and pain. Why had God allowed me to survive when others, like Tamir Rice, Oscar Grant, Sean Bell, Ezell Ford, Ryan Davis, Adrian Williams, Nicholas Thomas, Rashaad Brookins, and countless more, had died,—defenseless in a puddle of cold blood?

Why was I fortunate enough to see my family again when others didn't receive the same opportunity? Why would God allow me to survive just to wake up and learn I would never walk again? Why did God trust that I was strong enough to use my voice to speak for those who couldn't speak for themselves?

For years, I remained baffled, never truly able to understand why God had chosen me to endure such great adversity and why He trusted me to push through the pain.

It wasn't until I discovered the scripture Ephesians 6:10–13 that I was able to understand how and why I survived. Multiple shots had pierced my body; one bullet tore through the flesh on my forehead without entering my skull.

Another invasive bullet shattered my collarbone, followed by another that pierced my arm, causing nerve damage. Another bullet penetrated my hip. And two bullets penetrating my chest, one stopping mere centimeters from my heart. The other entered my spine, leaving me paralyzed.

After I was shot, people would say "Everything happens for a reason" and "What the devil meant for evil, God will turn around for your good." It all seemed so cliché, and it didn't make me feel any better about my circumstances. But through the scripture, I came to see that my destiny was written; everything I went through was purposeful. For the first time in my life, I felt like I could relate to something in the Bible.

I discovered the scripture in a song called "So Much Things to Say" by R&B singer Lauryn Hill before I knew where it originated. While I listened to the song, God found me exactly where I was, and he knew what I would be receptive to. In the song, Hill mentions that she doesn't come to fight flesh and blood but spiritual wickedness in high and low places. I thought those were simply lyrics, not an actual scripture from the bible.

The first time I read the scripture I was completely blown away. It felt as if God was revealing my purpose, my calling, and my destiny. The scripture informed me about my painful purpose, the enemy I was up against, how I should battle the enemy, and what the result would be. It felt like I had a premonition that allowed me to view the fullness of my life from a spiritual perspective.

Ephesians 6:10–13

10. Finally, be strong in the Lord and his mighty power. 11. Put on the full armor of God, so that you can take your stand against the devil's schemes.

This first scripture encouraged me, telling me to be strong and confident that the Lord is mighty. As I read further, I learned that by putting on the full armor God, He would protect me. I received foresight, letting me know that I would encounter evil and that things would happen to me, but when those things happened I had to trust that the armor of God was stronger than anything the devil might present to me.

It was this scripture that revealed to me that God didn't cause me pain; the devil did. But God gets the glory for bringing me out of the pain gracefully.

12. For we wrestle not against flesh and blood, but against principalities, against powers, against the rulers of the darkness of this world, against spiritual wickedness in high places.

After being unjustly shot, my initial inclination was to retaliate. I was angry, consumed by hatred. I felt as if I didn't have anything more to lose. But God revealed to me that I had a divine purpose. He blessed me with the wisdom to understand that there was no way I could win the battle with violence. The only way I would emerge victorious was by standing on truth and challenging those in positions of power.

The scripture served as confirmation that the system was indeed broken and those I was up against were wicked. Wrestling with flesh and blood would only make me just as wicked as those who'd caused me pain. The only way to stand up against principalities, powers, and rulers of the darkness in this world is through spiritual righteousness. Through spiritual righteousness, I am positive, honest, and pure, even when others have caused me pain. Now understanding that this is a spiritual battle, I constantly stay positive, even when anger and bitterness are the easier emotions to harvest.

13. Therefore put on the full armor of God, so that when the day of evil comes, you may be able to stand your ground, and after you have done everything, to stand.

Although I experienced an astronomical amount of pain, I was protected. No pain can penetrate the armor of God that always covers me. This scripture prepared me—spiritually, mentally, physically, and emotionally—for the things the enemy planned for me. The night I was unjustly shot and paralyzed, the evil done to me was intended to destroy me, but with the armor of God I survived to tell my story. I was shot, paralyzed, and charged with crimes I did not commit. Even though the media scrutinized me, leadership within my community let me down. I experienced a strenuous trial threatening my freedom. Even though I still fight for justice, I continue to stand on truth by confidently embracing my divine purpose.

The scripture confirmed that there would be not one but a series of challenging events. However, I wore the armor of God, trusting that God would always protect me and that no matter what I faced, I would always be victorious. One of the most compelling components of this scripture relates that even though I have been challenged to stand up against adversity and my process is painful, I know that there is a greater reward in the end.

The scripture clearly states "you may be able to stand your ground, and after you have done everything, to stand." The scripture lets me know that I will not only be able to stand up against spiritual wickedness, I will be victorious, and I will be given back everything I have lost, including my ability to walk.

As mentioned throughout this book, God will find you exactly where you are. When the spirit of God presents itself, it is solely up to you to be receptive. The benefits of being receptive to the spirit of God include being able to find peace in the midst of chaos, leading from a place of love, and viewing the fullness of your life from a spiritual perspective. No matter what attacks you experience, you will prevail.

Viewing the fullness of your life through a spiritual perspective requires faith. You must trust that even your lowest moments are meaningful in the grand scheme of things.

Daily Shift

As you navigate through life wearing the armor of God, be mindful of the following daily shifts:

1. God will find you exactly where you are, but it is up to you to be receptive.
2. Remember that you are alive for a reason; God trusts you to fulfill a purpose.
3. You will come under attack. However, be strong in the Lord and trust that he will always protect you.

Affirmation of Armor

The armor of God is powerful,
stronger than anything the devil may present to me.
I will wear my armor with confidence.
I will wear my armor with love.
I am stronger than my circumstances.
I am resilient.
I lead with love even when I am hated.
I will not become what has harmed me.
I will be prayerful.
I will be graceful.
I will be protected.
Through the Lord, I can handle any adversity that comes my way.

EPILOGUE

To my readers,

As long as you have breath in your body, you have the power to change any position you find yourself in. Step up with confidence, embrace your painful experiences, and trust God, because He is with you through every step of your process. Learn all that you can learn, because you're going to need knowledge for the journey. It may be difficult now, but it will get easier later. Be courageous; the only place to go is up. If you feel you have reached your lowest point, remember that you cannot fall off the floor.

Have faith and be hopeful, because everything that you've been through is purposeful. Trust God, because he will turn your tragedy into triumph. You have all the resources you need to be inspired, to be great, and to make your life purposeful. Don't become stuck in your pain. Being in pain hurts more than coming out of pain. So use all of your God-given strength to move beyond your pain. Trust your spirit; God will not forsake you. Do not be frustrated; your fatigue is just a sign that you must let go of some things so you can grow. Be mindful of what you let go of, and be intentional when you are called to let go. You must give up to go up.

Remember that you have God. Do not accept low self-esteem because of how people around you treat you; your life has meaning. Respect and love all lives, because we are all creations of the Most High and we all have purpose on this earth.

Remember that you are great; remember that your life is meaningful. Embrace your greatness; never limit yourself.

Be helpful, be intentional, be wise, be transparent—be you and be resilient. You have a calling, and God is with you every step of the way. Do not limit yourself. Remember that God has big plans for you. Just live. Live life, experience every moment, and be intentionally great. Stay motivated, be inspired, and keep inspiring people. Lead with love. Don't allow societal ills to change the goodness inside of you. Be pure, be prayerful, and keep God first.

Sincerely,
Leon Ford

LEON FORD LEGACY FUND

Leon Ford has dedicated his life to being a positive leader of social change. He understands the significance of philanthropy and he has made a commitment to use his platform to provide resources to causes, organizations and communities seeking philanthropic support.

The Leon Ford Legacy Fund was established in September 2017, to advocate for community healing, individual empowerment, and social change, with a specific focus of turning pain into purpose and transforming grief into greatness. Mr. Ford is excited about using his passion and platform to engage his network to support the Fund; and has identified these key areas of interest to support:

• Provide a "brave" space that can allow the community to tell their stories, to have courageous conversations, and to create strong solutions for their personal adversity.

• Invoke social change by encouraging the community to utilize their voice, construct and expand upon their unique platform for healing and social justice.

• Provide scholarships, networking and mentorship opportunities for students who have overcome adversity.

• Break down racial barriers through sharing and understanding personal stories.

• Facilitating and fostering close bonds and connections for social justice collaboration and community building.

• Support platforms for unique voices to be heard.

We proudly partner with POISE FOUNDATION to manage the Leon Ford Legacy Fund. The Fund has been established to help us expand our charitable work, including: scholarships for students seeking post-secondary educational experiences and; grants to organizations which support storytelling, mentorship, civic engagement and other activities, helping to turn tragedy into triumph. We encourage empowerment through creating opportunities for individuals to utilize the power of their voice to express themselves and to share their stories with others. We need and appreciate your support of the Fund! You can give to the fund by clicking the donate now button on www.leonfordspeaks.com

POISE FOUNDATION, a 501(C)3 charitable organization, began in December 1980 as the first public foundation in the state of Pennsylvania organized and managed by African Americans. POISE helps donors meet their philanthropic goals to support Black families, organizations and communities, through collective giving and building endowment funds. In turn, those dollars are used to provide funding to worthy organizations, students and causes across the United States. Through 2017, POISE has provided more than $10M of funding towards these efforts.

Online donations are processed through PayPal and are made directly to POISE. You may also send a donation via check or money order made payable to: POISE Foundation; Two Gateway Center, Suite 1700; 603 Stanwix Street; Pittsburgh, PA 15222, note LEON FORD LEGACY FUND in the memo section. All donations are
Please contact POISE's Development Staff at 412-281-4967, Ext 211 if you have any questions or concerns.